WRITING SKILLS CURRICULUM LIBRARY

# Ready-to-Use

# SENTENCE Activities

UNIT 2

## JACK UMSTATTER

Illustrations by Maureen Umstatter

THE CENTER FOR APPLIED
RESEARCH IN EDUCATION
West Nyack, New York 10994

Library of Congress Cataloging-in-Publication Data

Umstatter, Jack.
    Writing skills curriculum library / Umstatter, Jack.
      p.    cm.
    Contents: Unit 1. Ready-to-use word activities
    ISBN 0-87628-482-9
    1. English language—Composition and exercises—Study and teaching
(Secondary)—United States.   2  Education, Secondary—Activity
programs—United States.   I.  Title.
    LB1631.U49 1999
    808′.042′0712—dc21                                    99-21556
                                                           CIP

*Printed in the United States of America*

10  9  8  7  6  5  4  3  2


ISBN 0-87628-483-7

**ATTENTION:CORPORATIONS AND SCHOOLS**

The Center for Applied Research in Education books are available at quantity discounts with bulk purchase for educational, business, or sales promotional use. For information, please write to: Prentice Hall Career & Personal Development Special Sales, 240 Frisch Court, Paramus, NJ 07652. Please supply: title of book, ISBN number, quantity, how the book will be used, date needed.

**The Center for Applied Research
in Education**
West Nyack, NY 10994


http://www.phdirect.com

# DEDICATED

To my daughter, Kate, whose beauty, smile, and talents
make the world that much better.

# ACKNOWLEDGMENTS

Thanks to my wife, Chris, for her many hours of dedicated work in this subject and to my daughter, Maureen, for her artistic creativity.

Thanks again to Connie Kallback and Win Huppuch for their support and encouragement with this series.

Appreciation and thanks to Diane Turso for her meticulous development and copyediting and to Mariann Hutlak, production editor, for her tireless attention to this project.

A special thanks to my students, past and present, who inspire these ideas and activities.

Thanks to Terry from WISCO COMPUTING of Wisconsin Rapids, Wisconsin for his programs.

Definitions for certain words are taken from *Webster's New World Dictionary, Third College Edition* (New York: Simon & Schuster, Inc., 1988).

# ABOUT THE AUTHOR

Jack Umstatter has taught English on both the junior high and senior high school levels since 1972, and education and literature at Dowling College (Oakdale, New York) for the past nine years. He currently teaches English in the Cold Spring Harbor School District in New York.

Mr. Umstatter graduated from Manhattan College with a B.A. in English and completed his M.A. in English at S.U.N.Y.—Stony Brook. He earned his Educational Administration degree at Long Island University.

Mr. Umstatter has been selected Teacher of the Year several times and was elected to *Who's Who Among America's Teachers*. Most recently, he appeared in *Contemporary Authors*. Mr. Umstatter has taught all levels of secondary English classes including the Honors and Advanced Placement classes. As coach of the high school's Academic team, the Brainstormers, he led the team in capturing the Long Island and New York State championships when competing in the American Scholastic Competition Network National Tournament of Champions in Lake Forest, Illinois.

Mr. Umstatter's other publications include *Hooked on Literature!* (1994), *201 Ready-to-Use Word Games for the English Classroom* (1994), *Brain Games!* (1996), and *Hooked on English!* (1997), all published by The Center for Applied Research in Education.

# ABOUT THE WRITING SKILLS CURRICULUM LIBRARY

According to William Faulkner, a writer needs three things—experience, observation, and imagination. As teachers, we know that our students certainly have these essentials. Adolescents love to express themselves in different ways. Writing is undoubtedly one of these modes of expression. We stand before potential novelists, poets, playwrights, columnists, essayists, and satirists (no comment!). How to tap these possibilities is our task.

The six-unit *Writing Skills Curriculum Library* was created to help your students learn the elements of effective writing and enjoy the experience at the same time. This series of progressive, reproducible activities will instruct your students in the various elements of the writing process as it fosters an appreciation for the writing craft. These stimulating and creative activities also serve as skill reinforcement tools. Additionally, since the lesson preparation has already been done, you will be able to concentrate on guiding your students instead of having to create, develop, and sequence writing exercises.

- Unit 1, *Ready-to-Use Word Activities*, concentrates on the importance of word selection and exactness in the writing process. William Somerset Maugham said, "Words have weight, sound and appearance; it is only by considering these that you can write a sentence that is good to look at and good to listen to." Activities featuring connotations, denotations, prefixes, roots, suffixes, synonyms, antonyms, and expressions will assist your students in becoming more conscientious and selective "verbivores," as Richard Lederer would call them. Diction, syntax, and specificity are also emphasized here.

- The renowned essayist, philosopher, and poet, Ralph Waldo Emerson, commented on the necessity of writing effective sentences. He said, "For a few golden sentences we will turn over and actually read a volume of four or five hundred pages." Knowing the essentials of the cogent sentence is the focus of Unit 2, *Ready-to-Use Sentence Activities*. Here a thorough examination of subjects, predicates, complements, types of sentences, phrases, clauses, punctuation, capitalization, and agreement situations can be found. Problems including faulty subordination, wordiness, dangling modifiers, faulty transition, and ambiguity are also addressed within these activities.

- "Every man speaks and writes with the intent to be understood." Samuel Johnson obviously recognized the essence of an effective paragraph. Unit 3, *Ready-to-Use Paragraph Writing Activities*, leads the students through the steps of writing clear, convincing paragraphs. Starting with brainstorming techniques, these activities also emphasize the importance of developing effective thesis statements and topic sentences, selecting an appropriate paragraph form, organizing the paragraph, introducing the paragraph, utilizing relevant supporting ideas, and concluding the paragraph. Activities focusing on methods of developing a topic—description, exemplification, process, cause and effect, comparison-contrast, analogy, persuasion, and definition—are included.

- "General and abstract ideas are the source of the greatest errors of mankind." Jean-Jacques Rousseau's words befit Unit 4, *Ready-to-Use Prewriting & Organization Activities*, for here the emphasis is on gathering and using information intelligently. Activities include sources of information, categorization, topics and subtopics, summaries, outlines, details, thesis statements, term-paper ideas, and formats.

- "Most people won't realize that writing is a craft." Katherine Anne Porter's words could be the fifth unit's title. Unit 5, *Ready-to-Use Revision & Proofreading Activities*, guides the students through the problem areas of writing. Troublesome areas such as verb tense, words often confused, superfluity, double negatives, and clarity issues are presented in interesting and innovative ways. Students will become better proofreaders as they learn to utilize the same skills used by professional writers.

- "Our appreciation of fine writing will always be in proportion to its real difficulty and its apparent ease." Charles Caleb Colton must have been listening in as Unit 6, *Ready-to-Use Portfolio Development Activities*, was developed. Students are exposed to many different types of practical writings including literary analyses, original stories and sketches, narratives, reviews, letters, journal entries, newspaper articles, character analyses, dialogue writing, college admission essays, and commercials. The goal is to make the difficult appear easy!

Whether you use these realistic classroom-tested activities for introduction, remediation, reinforcement, or enrichment, they will guide your students toward more effective writing. Many of the activities include riddles, hidden words and sayings, word-finds, and other devices that allow students to check their own answers. These activities will also help you to assess your student's progress.

So go ahead and make Mr. Faulkner proud by awakening the experience, observation, and imagination of your students. The benefits will be both theirs—and yours!

*Jack Umstatter*

# ABOUT UNIT 2

*Ready-to-Use Sentence Activities*, the second unit in the *Writing Skills Curriculum Library*, includes 90 practical and enjoyable reproducible activities to help students write better and more interesting sentences. Many of these activities can be used as individual, small-group/cooperative learning, or entire-class activities. While some can serve as a ten– or fifteen–minute minilesson, others can fill a full thirty or more minutes of solid sentence writing. Use an activity as a test, quiz, homework or class competition, or to introduce or reinforce a concept. The applications are many! Some of the activities use riddles, hidden words, word-finds, quotations, and other devices that allow students to check their own answers.

• Activities 1 through 19, "Beginning with the Basics," guide students through the fundamentals of the sentence. The parts of speech, sentence terms and classifications, and specific types of sentences, including the topic sentence and the periodic sentence, are covered here.

• Activities 20 through 32, "Moving Onward and Upward," reinforce some of the sentence basics and introduce various methods of constructing sentences. Five activities are puzzles that will pique your students' interest.

• Activities 33 through 51, "Sentence Essentials," concentrate on the different types of phrases and clauses that help to build better sentences. Additionally, students learn how to avoid writing fragments and run-ons, two common writing errors. These fun and challenging activities will help your students write more interesting and convincing sentences.

• Activities 52 through 63, "Improving Your Sentences," offer exercises in editing the sentences to show how to write more concise and intelligent sentences. Activities dealing with words often confused, idioms, similes, and clichés help the students to write fresher, more powerful sentences.

• Activities 64 through 76, "Shaping Sensational Sentences," help students construct different types of sentences. Combining many of the ideas featured in the previous sections, these activities allow students to enrich their sentences.

• Activities 77 through 90, "Writing More Maturely," lead students through the process of writing more advanced sentences. Beginning with three activities focusing on a sentence's most effective word order, this section also features six activities dealing with conjunctions and other transitions necessary for building more mature sentences.

These 90 classroom-tested activities will help your students learn more about the sentence and improve their sentence writing. Plus, the students will enjoy themselves as they learn! Write on!

*Jack Umstatter*

# CONTENTS

## SECTION ONE
## BEGINNING WITH THE BASICS

## SECTION TWO
# MOVING ONWARD AND UPWARD

## SECTION THREE
# SENTENCE ESSENTIALS

# SECTION FOUR
# IMPROVING YOUR SENTENCES

# SECTION FIVE
# SHAPING SENSATIONAL SENTENCES

# SECTION SIX
# WRITING MORE MATURELY

CONTENTS

# TEACHER'S CORRECTION MARKS

| | | | |
|---|---|---|---|
| ab | abbreviation problem | pr ref | pronoun reference problem |
| agr | agreement problem | pun | punctuation needed or missing |
| amb | ambiguous | | |
| awk | awkward expression or con-struction | reas | reasoning needs improve-ment |
| cap | capitalize | rep | unnecessary repetition |
| case | error in case | RO | run-on |
| cp | comma problem | shift | faulty tense shift |
| cs | comma splice | sp | incorrect spelling |
| d | inappropriate diction | thesis | improve the thesis |
| det | details are needed | trans | improve the transition |
| dm | dangling modifier | TX | topic sentence needed (or improved) |
| dn | double negative | | |
| frag | fragment | U | usage problem |
| ital | italics or underline | UW | unclear wording |
| lc | use lower case | V | variety needed |
| mm | misplaced modifier | VAG | vague |
| num | numbers problem | VE | verb error |
| ^ | insert | VT | verb tense problem |
| ¶ | new paragraph needed | w | wordy |
| ‖ | faulty parallelism | WC | better word choice |
| , | insert comma | WM | word missing |
| pass | misuse of passive voice | WW | wrong word |

# BEGINNING WITH THE BASICS

# 2-1. WHAT WILL A MOUSE DO?

Sentences are classified according to their purpose. A declarative sentence makes a statement. An imperative sentence makes a command or request. An interrogative sentence asks a question. An exclamatory sentence expresses strong feeling.

In the space next to the question's number, write the letter **T** if it is a **declarative** sentence, **A** if it is an **interrogative** sentence, **C** if it is an **imperative** sentence, and **R** if it is an **exclamatory** sentence. If your answers are correct, the letters will spell out a 3-word response to the question "What will a mouse do?" End punctuation marks have been purposely omitted.

1. _____ Will Jonah go to the movies with us

2. _____ The show is about to begin

3. _____ Most of the actors in that movie are famous people

4. _____ I am absolutely appalled by that behavior

5. _____ Am I the only one in the group who knows where you live

6. _____ Call me if you think you will be able to go with us

7. _____ Rico and Marilyn will go in your car

8. _____ Aren't they driving you there, Mitch

9. _____ Please check to see what time the movie ends

10. _____ Did you not ask them to go with us

11. _____ This is going to be a fun night

What will a mouse do? _____

On the other side of this sheet, write three example sentences for each of these four types of sentences. Share your sentences with your classmates.

# 2-2. THREE OF A KIND

How well do you know your grammar? What is the difference between an adverb and an adjective or the difference between a dependent clause and an independent clause? Here is your chance to show what you know.

Each item is found 3 times within the 10 sentences. Write the corresponding number above the underlined portion of the sentence.

| | |
|---|---|
| (1) article | (6) adverb |
| (2) adjective | (7) prepositional phrase |
| (3) subject | (8) direct object |
| (4) helping verb | (9) indirect object |
| (5) main verb | (10) dependent clause |

1. The man in the blue suit is my father's best friend.

2. The doctor slowly handed me the instrument near the machine.

3. Those who forget the past will be in trouble in the future.

4. Each of the people in the room knows your sister's fame.

5. The talented architect who designed this city gained lasting fame because of his feat.

6. Lately I have not been feeling well and think I should see a doctor.

7. The painting that is hanging in the adjacent room was a gift to the embassy.

8. He gave me a chance to take the last shot in the game.

9. An intelligent decision must be made immediately in this case.

10. Justin will be studying physical therapy for the next three years.

# 2-3. LOOKING INTO THE HEART OF THE SENTENCE

*Thrilled with her performance in these final events, the skilled gymnast, who had scored well last year, waited for three judges to tally their scores.*

Each of the 25 words in this sentence is an answer in the crossword puzzle. Fill in the correct word for each clue. No word is used more than once.

**ACROSS**

4. noun that ends the participial phrase
6. adjective
7. main verb of the dependent clause
8. the final word in the adjectival clause
9. main verb of the independent clause
11. subject of the independent clause
13. verb in the infinitive phrase
14. word describing *year*
15. helping verb of the dependent clause
17. the second pronoun/adjective found in the participial phrase
18. relative pronoun
19. noun ending the infinitive phrase
20. the participial phrase's initial word

**DOWN**

1. adverb
2. object of the first prepositional phrase
3. a preposition
5. an article
6. preposition
7. adjective meaning more than competent
10. noun meaning those who make decisions
12. numerical adjective
13. plural pronoun/adjective
16. the sentence's initial pronoun/adjective
17. word beginning the infinitive phrase
18. alphabetically, the last preposition

# 2-4. THE TERMS OF THE SENTENCE

Twenty-five terms associated with a sentence are your answers in this crossword puzzle. Fill in the correct answers to these clues.

**ACROSS**

1. a group of words that serves as a single part of speech; it does not contain a subject and a verb
6. verb form, usually ending in -ed or -ing, that is sometimes used as an adjective
7. type of sentence that makes a statement
11. joins words or ideas
13. modifies adjectives, verbs, and adverbs
16. word indicating one
18. type of noun that names a specific person, place, thing, or idea
19. an action word
20. type of sentence that consists of a single main clause and no subordinate clause
21. type of sentence that consists of a main clause and one or more subordinating clauses
22. type of sentence that asks a question

**DOWN**

2. *a*, *an*, and *the* are examples of this type of adjective
3. type of verb that expresses a state of being
4. type of verb that ends in -ing and acts as a noun
5. a group of words that contains a subject and a verb
6. takes the place of a noun
8. type of sentence that expresses strong feeling
9. two or more sentences incorrectly punctuated as one
10. part of speech that expresses emotion
12. type of sentence that consists of two or more main clauses and no subordinate clause
13. modifies a noun or a pronoun
14. a verbal consisting of *to* plus a verb
15. type of sentence that makes a request or gives a command
17. an incomplete sentence
18. word indicating more than one

# 2-5. FITTING THE PIECES TOGETHER

Match the sentences in Group One with their grammatical descriptions in Group Two. Write the appropriate letters from Group Two on the line next to its counterpart in Group One. If your answers are correct, the letters will spell out a word and its antonym.

## Group One

1. _____   The old man walked slowly down the beach with his dog.

2. _____   Bob and Carol walk together at the mall after supper.

3. _____   None of the bread was left on the counter.

4. _____   At the start of the semester, the students are eager to meet their teachers.

5. _____   The package that you found belongs to Joanne.

6. _____   Saving his best effort for the final event, the discus thrower set the record for the meet.

7. _____   The group slowly walked around the museum.

8. _____   Neither Ted nor Linda saw that the light had changed.

## Group Two

The sentence contains (among other components):

(cu) an indefinite pronoun subject, two prepositional phrases, verb phrase

(lo) two prepositional phrases, an infinitive phrase, plural subject

(me) a common noun subject, an adverb, two prepositional phrases, and a past tense verb

(op) collective noun subject, adverb, prepositional phrase

(py) singular subjects joined by conjunctions, noun clause

(sl) participial phrase, past tense verb

(ti) compound subject, present tense verb, adverb, two prepositional phrases

(us) adjective clause, prepositional phrase

Word: _____   Antonym: _____

# 2-6. PUTTING IT ALL TOGETHER

Now that you have the basics, it is time to put it all together. Different types of sentences, phrases, and clauses are familiar to you. Let's see how well you can blend these elements into a composition. Starting on the lines below and continuing on the other side, use these nine elements to form a well-written composition. An example of each element is given to you; however, do not use these specific examples in your original composition.

**Participial phrase:** <u>Walking down the lonely, dimly lit road,</u> the stranger felt uneasy.

**Gerund phrase:** <u>Walking down the lonely road</u> was scary for the stranger.

**Infinitive phrase:** The stranger did not want <u>to walk down the lonely road</u>.

**Adjective phrase:** The man <u>with the baseball cap</u> is his coach.

**Adverb phrase:** The man ran ten miles <u>in the evening</u>.

**Noun clause:** <u>What I wanted</u> was not considered by the group.

**Adjective clause:** Johnny was dating Marilyn, <u>who is the smartest one in our class</u>.

**Adverb clause:** <u>Before you go away</u>, visit Grandma.

**Appositive phrase:** Tennessee, <u>the Volunteer State</u>, is a scenic state.

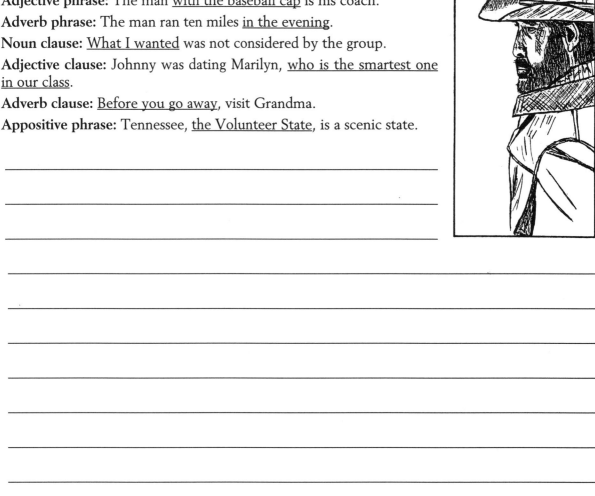

_____

_____

_____

_____

_____

_____

_____

_____

_____

_____

© 1999 by The Center for Applied Research in Education

# 2-7. WE HAVE ATTITUDES! 15 OF THEM!

The skilled writer knows that a topic sentence needs a subject and an attitude toward that subject. In the sentence "This was the most memorable day of my life," the topic is *day* and the attitude is *memorable*. If the writer were to continue the paragraph, he or she would have to explain why the day was memorable. This is how effective paragraphs are written.

In this activity you are given an attitude and are asked to construct a sentence expressing that attitude. So if the attitude were "beneficial," a possible sentence could read, "This summer's Outdoors Program was helpful for developing students' self-confidence." On the line following each attitude, write a sentence illustrating that attitude. Share your sentences with your classmates.

1. sensational _____

2. awesome _____

3. confusing _____

4. remarkable _____

5. perfect _____

6. stupendous _____

7. unforgettable _____

8. frightening _____

9. extraordinary _____

10. disastrous _____

11. terrible _____

12. uninspiring _____

13. best _____

14. motivational _____

15. boring _____

# 2-8. MOOD SENTENCES

On the line below each group of sentences, write the mood you feel the author is trying to convey. Circle the words, phrases, and other elements that contribute to the prevalent mood. Discuss your answers with your classmates.

1. I could barely feel my legs, and my heart was pumping madly as I awaited the news of my grandfather's operation. He had been in the operating room for the past four hours, and I had been in the hospital's waiting room with the other members of my family.

   _____

2. Both people could hardly bear the silence pervading the room. Never before had the married couple said such hurtful words to one another.

   _____

3. This was not how she had planned spending her sixteenth birthday. Snowbound in a Midwestern airport unable to even call her friends back home was both painful and irritating. What else could go wrong now? She anxiously awaited the next calamity.

   _____

4. Maybe it was a joke, some playful scheme they worked out. Maybe it was not. Either way, the present moment was frightening, eerie, and unwarranted. Within the next ten minutes, she would know the truth.

   _____

5. The coach was the first to enter the locker room. She quietly waited for the players to arrive. Losing on the last play of the game was difficult. Addressing her dejected players would be even more unpleasant.

   _____

6. Mrs. Osbourne, the chemistry teacher, had told the class that tomorrow's test would be very difficult. Slumped over her notebook, Krissy was exhausted from these past four hours of intensive studying. Her hair was messy, her nails were badly bitten, and her eyes were bloodshot.

   _____

Now write three of your own examples and see if your classmates can guess the mood you are trying to convey.

© 1999 by The Center for Applied Research in Education

# 2-9. THE PERIODIC SENTENCE

Talented writers use variety in their sentence structure. They combine short sentences with longer ones. One technique they employ is the periodic sentence, a sentence that adds details inside a basic statement. In a periodic sentence, the original sentence is divided in two in order to add more information. Thus, the original sentence "Larry is an exceptional athlete" becomes a periodic sentence by adding information such as "Larry, *the center on our school's basketball team and an All-State first-team selection*, is an exceptional athlete."

Change the following ten original sentences into periodic sentences. Write your new sentences on the lines. Share your answers with your classmates.

1. The weather has been unusual. _____
   _____

2. Our car is an eyesore. _____
   _____

3. Mrs. Haley was elated. _____
   _____

4. The new CD is the group's best combination of songs. _____
   _____

5. The team is exceptional. _____
   _____

6. *Seventeen* is an interesting magazine. _____
   _____

7. My job is pretty boring. _____
   _____

8. The kindergarten children enjoyed spending time with us. _____
   _____

9. The movie is funny. _____
   _____

10. Our neighborhood is unique. _____
   _____

# 2-10. A STARTER SENTENCE'S PURPOSE

The sentence that starts your story or essay is an important one. It sets the stage for what comes after it. Facts and opinions regarding characters, settings, actions, moods, and more are presented to the reader beginning with the piece's opening line. Established authors know the significance of the story starter. Its purpose cannot be underestimated.

On the lines following these 10 opening sentences, write the purpose of each opener. Does it establish character? Set a mood? Relate action? Create suspense? Something else? Discuss your answers with your classmates.

1. Like a ravenously hungry dog awaiting its prey, the soldier stood watch over the enemy's path that night.

   _____

2. For the first twenty years of our lives, my wife and I lived a block away from each other, but we never even knew it!

   _____

3. The Cape Cod sunset made this most solemn occasion even more memorable.

   _____

4. Muhammad Ali, maybe the most recognized person on the planet, continues to inspire the many who have thought about giving up on life.

   _____

5. It was the singularly most detestable act ever committed by one human being upon another, and unfortunately, I was there to witness it.

   _____

6. Tonight when you place your head upon your fluffy pillow, dream of the glorious days of kings, queens, knights, and castles.

   _____

7. Laughing hysterically, the three college freshmen on Christmas vacation, friends who had known each other since the first day of high school, sat in Maureen's bedroom relating stories about their new friends and experiences at college.

   _____

8. I traveled back to my old neighborhood in Brooklyn and found it tremendously different from when I moved away some twenty years ago.

   _____

9. I first heard about the reclusive actress from the doorman at her posh Manhattan hotel and somehow wish I had never been privy to this bit of gossip.

   _____

# 2-11. STRENGTHENING YOUR SENTENCES

Starting with the base sentence, add the suggested additions to the sentence. Write the new sentences that are more colorful, detailed, and interesting on the lines provided.

1. Jerry spoke. (*Add two prepositional phrases, two adverbs, and two adjectives.*)

   _____

   _____

2. The cheetah ran. (*Add a prepositional phrase, a participial phrase, and an adjective.*)

   _____

   _____

3. A car passed us. (*Add a color, a time, and an "-ly" word.*)

   _____

   _____

4. The soccer player walked with her teammate. (*Add an adjective, another verb, a prepositional phrase, and a subordinate clause.*)

   _____

   _____

5. My sister traveled to Europe. (*Add a conjunction, an additional subject of the sentence, an adjective, a pronoun/adjective, and a prepositional phrase.*)

   _____

   _____

6. The movie is exciting. (*Add a conjunction, two adjectives, and an adjectival clause.*)

   _____

   _____

7. She did yesterday's crossword puzzle. (*Add a prepositional phrase, an adverb, and replace the dull verb "did."*)

   _____

   _____

8. The wind was strong. The umbrella blew over. (*Combine these two sentences using a subordinate clause.*)

   _____

   _____

9. We saw the vehicle. (*Replace "vehicle" with a more specific word; replace "We" with two pronouns and a conjunction; add an adjective.*)

   _____

   _____

10. He was the last man. (*Add an infinitive phrase and replace "He" with a specific name.*)

    _____

    _____

# 2-12. COP AN ATTITUDE

A good topic sentence contains a subject and an attitude toward that subject. It is not a statement of fact. Instead, it attempts to persuade the reader's opinion toward the subject matter. A topic sentence is specific and directed. Thus, the topic sentence "Bargain hunting is challenging" is effective because it contains a topic, *bargain hunting*, and an opinion or attitude, *challenging*, toward the subject matter.

Circle the topic and underline the attitude in these 15 sentences. You may be circling and underlining more than a single word for a particular answer.

1. My mother is a very interesting woman.

2. The rock group's performance at the stadium was outrageous.

3. Our honored speaker at last year's graduation ceremony offered inspirational words to our seniors.

4. Spending all that money on a new car seems rather foolish to Grandpa.

5. The movie was boring.

6. His presentation of the new material was soporific.

7. She is a very efficient office manager.

8. Trying to convince his mother to allow him to go skiing with his friends that weekend was an exercise in futility.

9. His response to our question was shocking.

10. *The New York Times* contains many intellectually stimulating articles.

11. Mr. Bergen's health class is challenging.

12. The mosquitoes' infestation has been an annoyance for the local homeowners.

13. Laurie's way of looking at the situation is strange.

14. Driving to work each morning is very taxing for Tom.

15. Marie has an uncanny method of taking care of matters.

© 1999 by The Center for Applied Research in Education

Name _____  Date _____  Period _____

# 2-13. MAKING OBSERVATIONS

Authors describe their characters by keenly observing these people. What are they wearing? What are they saying? How are they walking or talking? Do they have a peculiar mannerism? These are just some of the questions authors think of as they describe characters to the reader.

Describe four people you see today. On the lines indicated, answer the questions about these people. Be as detailed and exact as possible. Instead of saying simply, "He is wearing a sweater," you could say, "The tall, handsome man wore a blue, woolen sweater." Your answers do not have to be in complete sentences.

Describe the physical appearance of Person # 1: _____

_____

Describe the clothing of Person # 1: _____

_____

Describe what you saw Person # 1 doing: _____

_____

Describe the physical appearance of Person # 2: _____

_____

Describe the clothing of Person # 2: _____

_____

Describe what you saw Person # 2 doing: _____

_____

Describe the physical appearance of Person # 3: _____

_____

Describe the clothing of Person # 3: _____

_____

Describe what you saw Person # 3 doing: _____

_____

Describe the physical appearance of Person # 4: _____

_____

Describe the clothing of Person # 4: _____

_____

Describe what you saw Person # 4 doing: _____

_____

# 2-14. DESCRIPTIONS OF PEOPLE

Three paragraphs describing people appear below. Circle the words that help you picture these characters. Then on the lines below the people descriptions, tell what effect the author is trying to achieve? Additionally, list the strategies employed by the author including effective adjectives, adverbs, comparisons, and contrasts. Discuss your answers with your classmates.

She was larger than life itself with her tall frame, keen eyes, and commanding presence. Her elegant clothes bought in the finest Fifth Avenue shops set her apart from the others. Entering the exquisite room, she was the focus of attention on this grandest of nights.

_____

_____

_____

Hank Smith, the sole boiler mechanic for the Wather's Manufacturing Company, wiped his gray-bearded lined face as he took a needed moment's rest from the unenviable task of cleaning yet another of the factory's antiquated, soot-filled boilers. Hank, with his gnarled hands, dirt-caked fingernails, and wrinkled forehead, had been repairing and cleaning boilers for as long as any of the factory workers could remember.

_____

_____

_____

Her ninety-nine years had left their marks on Louise's body, but not on her mind and spirit. A hearing aid, worn initially against her will, helped her to carry on conversations about the past century. Now a bit stooped and slower than twenty-five years ago, she usually walked with the help of her cane and a caring relative. Though she had buried three of her five children, she found solace in the presence of her grandchildren, great grandchildren, and great-great grandchildren. She was the talk of her small New England community.

_____

_____

_____

On the back of this page, write two people descriptions of your own. Share your descriptions with a classmate or two.

© 1999 by The Center for Applied Research in Education

# 2-15. MORE DESCRIPTIONS OF PEOPLE

For this description activity choose five people. They can be relatives, friends, acquaintances, celebrities, or fictional characters. For each person, list five adjectives that describe that person well. Then in either two or three sentences, no more or no less, include those five descriptive adjectives in a mini-paragraph about that person. An example is given to you.

**Person:** <u>Uncle Herbie</u> **Adjectives:** <u>tall, intelligent, humorous, sensitive, and athletic</u>
Uncle Herbie, a humorous guy also has a very sensitive side to him. Tall and athletic, Herbie is one of the most intelligent people I have ever met.

Person: _____ Adjectives: _____

_____

_____

_____

Person: _____ Adjectives: _____

_____

_____

_____

Person: _____ Adjectives: _____

_____

_____

_____

Person: _____ Adjectives: _____

_____

_____

_____

Person: _____ Adjectives: _____

_____

_____

_____

# 2-16. POETIC DESCRIPTIONS

Writers know the importance of good description. They strive to create accurate and meaningful descriptions to help the reader understand the character, mood, setting, or situation. The clearer the description, the better the reader's perception of the writer's intentions.

   Most of the following 3-line poems have requirements, including a goal. Some of the 3 lines are left blank. Write your own words following the specifications. The first one is done for you. There can be many different answers for these requirements. Share your answers with your classmates.

1. *goal:* **create a mood of sadness**
   _____cold_____, ____lonely____, and ____abandoned____ (*three adjectives*)
   _in a remote forest___ (*phrase*)
   _a baby wolf_____ (*subject of the two previous lines*)

2. *goal:* **create a mood of tranquillity**
   _____ and _____ (*adjectives*)
   on a summer's evening (*phrase*)
   _____ (*place*)

3. *goal:* **create a mood of comfort**
   _____, _____, and
   _____ (*adjectives*)
   _____ (*time*)
   my grandmother's house (*place*)

4. *goal:* **create a mood of discomfort**
   _____, _____, and
   _____ (*adjectives*)
   on this humid June afternoon (*time*)
   _____ (*event*)

5. *goal:* **create a mood of disgust**
   _____ and _____ (*adjectives*)
   _____ (*time*)
   the city's train terminal (*place*)

6. *goal:* **create a memorable experience**
   cool, beautiful, and exciting (*adjectives*)
   _____ (*time*)
   _____ (*place*)

7. *goal:* **describe a memorable person**
   _____, _____, and _____ (*adjectives*)
   on the concert stage (*location*)
   _____ (*person*)

8. *goal:* **describe a literary character**
   _____ and _____ (*adjectives*)
   _____ (*your choice*)
   _____ (*character's name*)

# 2-17. MAKING SENSE (AND SENTENCES) OUT OF POETRY

Paraphrase these poetic excerpts. Using clear and concise sentences, write your interpretations on the lines following each poetic excerpt. Compare your answers with those of your classmates.

1.  Never hath the sun risen so sneakily,
    Nor the moon left so quietly.
    Day and night confused each other.

    _____

    _____

2.  Heaven has sent the warning.
    Man must heed its sign.
    The bells tell its purpose.
    Beware, the time is here.

    _____

    _____

3.  She sits by the window watching the people pass by.
    A long time ago she was one of them.
    Shy and silly she was then,
    But how time has changed all that today!

    _____

    _____

4.  Wrinkles, the sands of human time, do not belie.
    They appear when the day's done or the sun's risen.
    Do not cry about these lines, Nature's markings,
    For they add to thine beauty, my lady fair.

    _____

    _____

5.  The nightingale and the lark confused Romeo and Juliet,
    But they will not do the same to you and me.
    I have studied the nightingale in the woods and the lark in the tree
    And neither bird will make a dodo out of me!

    _____

    _____

© 1999 by The Center for Applied Research in Education

# 2-18. STRUCTURING YOUR SENTENCES

Sentences are structured by function and structure. Here you will practice structuring your sentences using simple, compound, complex, and compound–complex sentences. Follow the directions to combine the original sentences. An example is done for you.

**Example:** Georgia is a southern state. It borders Florida. (*simple*)
Georgia is a southern state bordering Florida. _____

1. A new family moved into our neighborhood. The family has four young children. (*complex*)
_____
_____

2. The church's steeple is quite high. The roofer had a difficult time nailing the shingles on the church's steeple. (*complex*)
_____
_____

3. Walking to the park takes a long time. Walking to the park is good exercise. (*compound*)
_____
_____

4. The Hudsons broke down on the highway. The tow truck arrived 30 minutes later. They paid the driver 70 dollars to tow them back to his garage. (*compound-complex*)
_____
_____

5. Those trees are weeping willows. The weeping willows give good shade. (*simple*)
_____
_____

6. The doctor told us the good news. Then we celebrated. (*compound*)
_____
_____

7. Our desk drawer was messy. We could not find the license application. We had to go to the county office for another application. (*compound–complex*)
_____
_____

8. The weather was almost unbearable. We had two air conditioners and three fans working in our house. (*simple*)
_____
_____

9. His stapler was jammed. He could not staple his term paper's 12 pages together. (*complex*)
_____
_____

10. His stapler was jammed. He could not staple his term paper's 12 pages. (*compound*)
_____
_____

# 2-19. HOW SIMPLE? HOW COMPOUND? HOW COMPLEX?

Sentences are classified by function and by structure. This activity focuses on the sentence's structure. Using the abbreviations indicated, tell whether the sentence is simple (S), compound (CPD), complex (CPLX), or compound–complex (CC). Write the corresponding abbreviations on the correct lines. If your answers are correct, each type of sentence will be represented three times. The totals of the answers for each sentence type are as follows: simple (21), compound (22), complex (17), and compound–complex (18).

1. _____ Kenny's driver's license was lost when he left his wallet at the beach.

2. _____ My first-grade teacher was caring, and my second-grade teacher was humorous.

3. _____ Even though the bus broke down, the students waited quietly, and their chaperones appreciated their patience.

4. _____ The Rocky Mountains are both breath-taking and picturesque.

5. _____ None of the coaches who had coached Robert forgot him.

6. _____ After you have completed college, attend graduate school, and then the job offers will probably be more numerous.

7. _____ Can you believe this beautiful climate here in San Diego?

8. _____ Both countries have very interesting cultures, and we should learn to appreciate their customs.

9. _____ Since the noisy trains that were passing by could be heard from our campsite, we decided to move to another location, and the rest of the group quickly agreed with our plan.

10. _____ How could you ever think that of me, Ned?

11. _____ Ontario is the province that we would like to visit this summer.

12. _____ Last Tuesday, the heat forced the elderly to stay indoors, and the apartment complex's air conditioners were forced to work extra hard.

# MOVING ONWARD AND UPWARD

# 2-20. STAYING SIMPLE FOR STARTERS

By definition, a simple sentence has a single main (or independent) clause. A simple sentence must have a subject and a predicate. The words "The light in the kitchen was shining through the curtain" is a simple sentence.

Underline the first letter of the subject and the main verb in each sentence. Then write those letters, in order, at the bottom of this page. If the consecutive letters form a question and its answer, you have correctly identified each subject and verb!

1. The warden handed the prisoner a towel.

2. All of the soldiers talked about the strenuous drills.

3. The song took me back to the days of my youth.

4. The hawk quickly elevated itself toward the mountains.

5. War overtook the small foreign town.

6. The boy's sad realization lingered for days.

7. The days speed by.

8. The skilled linguist articulated the phrases beautifully.

9. That particular region of the state generated much revenue.

10. The estimates of our treasurer seem reasonable.

11. The three of us called each other last night.

12. The ovation numbed the young opera singer.

13. Thinking intrigues the sharpest minds.

14. None of those birds will eat that food.

15. The nonconformist has traveled alone quite often.

16. The quick ascent of the jet scared the infant.

17. Does the investigation astound you?

Write the letters here: _____

# 2-21. MAIN VERBS

Underline the main verb in each sentence below. Then write the word in the proper space within the crossword puzzle.

**ACROSS**

3. A young girl had been stung by a swarm of bees.
8. How long has the lake been frozen?
9. Nobody had caught the joke the teacher cracked.
12. The window was broken by the prankster.
13. I have known you for at least seven years.
15. They should have seen the difference.
16. The team was beaten by fourteen points.
17. They have never lost their goodness.

**DOWN**

1. Ethan Frome had ridden on his sled many times.
2. Two pipes had burst during the cold spell.
4. You have grown at least three inches in the past two years.
5. She was led to believe that it would be all right.
6. None of the machines will run smoothly.
7. The accident victim was visibly shaken.
8. The rushing boy flung his coat near the chair.
9. A cat had crept along the rafter yesterday.
10. Has she ever gone this route before today?
11. Have you gotten your flu shot?
12. He had borne the problems of the family.
14. Hadn't I lent that book to you earlier?

# 2-22. LIFE'S BIG QUESTION

Underline the subject and circle the main verb of each sentence's main clause (some sentences have only a main clause). Then write the subject's first letter followed by the main verb's first letter on the line at the bottom of this sheet. If you are correct, you will have spelled out the words in Life's Big Question. The first sentence is already done for you.

1. The <u>workers</u> (offered) us several options regarding the room's design.

2. Many colorful umbrellas lined the shore yesterday.

3. A driver was yelling at the pedestrian for walking in front of his car.

4. The court officers really understood the judge's wishes.

5. Last night the raccoon suddenly attacked the young animal.

6. The temperature has already hit more than 100 degrees.

7. In his eulogy the earl recounted several interesting stories about the deceased member of the royal family.

8. The boom echoed throughout the canyon.

9. At approximately 10:30 the harbor emptied quite quickly.

10. Two or three thousand airplanes landed within minutes of each other.

11. That tragedy happened four years ago.

12. You had already offered to do that for your sister.

13. Theresa's recorder worked beautifully during the assembly.

14. Each of the twelve jurors accepted the ruling without question.

15. After reading Mary's letter, Leroy told us that Mary's family was moving back to our neighborhood.

16. Their team's best hitter yelled after she was hit by the pitch.

Life's big question: <u>Wo</u>_____?

# 2-23. PARTS-OF-SPEECH TRIOS

In this activity each of the eight parts of speech is an answer 3 times. Use the following abbreviations for each part of speech: noun (n), pronoun (p), verb (v), adjective (adj), adverb (adv), preposition (prep), conjunction (c), and interjection (i). Write your answer on the line after the question's number.

1. _____ herself

2. _____ into

3. _____ ambled

4. _____ small

5. _____ country

6. _____ graphically

7. _____ between

8. _____ you

9. _____ nor

10. _____ is

11. _____ furtively

12. _____ and

13. _____ James

14. _____ yipee

15. _____ slowly

16. _____ hey

17. _____ wow

18. _____ or

19. _____ wonderful

20. _____ braggart

21. _____ has

22. _____ realistic

23. _____ during

24. _____ them

# 2-24. FIVE EACH

Five nouns, five pronouns, five verbs, five adjectives, and five adverbs are hidden in this word-find puzzle. Circle the 25 words that have been placed backward, forward, diagonally, and vertically. After you have circled each word, write its part of speech on the line next to it. Then you should have "five each"!

```
R D V P G W C S W Y C V Q K M R T L P X S J B Z
F C X Q T B V K O Y B L C D S L S Y S B J Z N B
P H V N H D W C D L N A D M K J V T H Z P T X N
R V K K E D K S K E I M U N G W R V R B F B K M
Z R F B M R L R K Y V D R T J R C S E O V R Z M
X N T L S F J T M Q S I L E O Q O Z Q R N A A Y
M I N T E L L I G E N T L Y W M M W Y K Y G R B
I K S M L S J F J A Z Q E I C A O N T F A M E Z
N T Q P V C R V S V N H D F S N R B I Z H S Q S
E I N F E S T U O Z T G S L D H D D I R O Y U H
H H R P S A O S O N L C R E T L I N E L L U I C
C D G Q M U K Q C Y D R R Y C L E T V N E K R X
F G D L N K K E X D L F N Q O B U D O F F W E S
X Y R E D X N P R T U R C S J P L G Q Z V H H H
Q G R N S X V D Q L C V Z B M X V R R B R B X N
D T V X J D R Z L R R J N O D K P Z R N Z M R H
S V Z N T Q G Z V C R J C B P D K K B P L Z N J
```

ANGRY _____   REQUIRE _____
AUTOMOBILE _____   SO _____
BRAG _____   SOLIDIFY _____
COMPUTER _____   SOLIDLY _____
DEVILISH _____   SPEAKER _____
DRAWER _____   STRENUOUS _____
GROW _____   STRONG _____
INFEST _____   THEMSELVES _____
INTELLIGENTLY _____   THEY _____
MAGAZINE _____   VERY _____
MINE _____   WONDERFUL _____
ONLY _____   YOURSELF _____
OURS _____

# 2-25. DOUBLE-DUTY WORDS

Each of the 40 words in this word-find puzzle can be used as both a verb and a noun. Circle the 40 words and then be prepared to show how each can function as those two parts of speech. The words are placed backward, forward, diagonally, and vertically.

```
D W M F Y S M Q D M H C V T C K K T S W T D V V
Y N W W C H I P S E Q X G S I J X E Q N N V S V
W P S C L S R B M N L S W K X D S L L U B J S V
V Q C C K O R L R T L S T L N A E U O O C L V F
Q T B U R R O W P I C K K A C T M R E W O L F L
H G L Q J O R K A O E W L W L X G A C O L H E P
S D A G P Q D N L N D F Y A F L W M F Q O V C S
N M B P N Z H D B Z G F N R R J L B D X R A A S
Y R E T T I L G N O S E N S E M E L R P F C F B
H B L L N Q R P C E O B C V W V N E A G I U S L
M Y M T L Q R P H F L K L Y I E M G W F N U L G
P K Z G M R W R S Y F B N R R M L W Z Z D M D W
C X D C D B L Y T B C F D K A J J L X M Y W Y G
C G R R X F K P Y M Y X R H F P R G K Z W P N D
T M A Q X B Y Y L L S Y B K Y H Z X D W M N R B
B U H M G C N Z L N N L W W T Z C Z Z Y B K W T
G W H T R P L H Y Z M D V C M W M S X L B H R Z
```

| | | | |
|---|---|---|---|
| ACT | DRIVE | HINT | RAMBLE |
| ARM | FACE | LABEL | RULE |
| BLEND | FALL | LAND | SCHOOL |
| BOOK | FIND | LOOK | SENSE |
| BRIEF | FLOWER | MENTION | SMELL |
| BURROW | FOOL | MIRROR | SPRING |
| CASE | GLITTER | NAIL | STALL |
| COLOR | GROUND | NOSE | SWELL |
| CREDIT | GUARD | PICK | VACUUM |
| DRAW | HAMMER | POOL | WALK |

# 2-26. SENTENCE ASSOCIATES

The 27 terms listed below are associated with a sentence. The terms are placed backward, forward, diagonally, and vertically. Circle each term, and then define it on the back of this sheet.

```
I N T E R J E C T I O N I M P E R A T I V E P M
N W R V H G M Y O S K R Q X Y V X V N D X F R L
F O Z I Z S E K Q M F H N Y V I F P O X F C E H
I R B T S W G R T N P C W N Q T Y V M Y G N P Q
N D M A S U Z D U X M O H Z B A S D I X T N O L
I S N G M H B G T N C K U F H R J R N D S S S H
T K L O D C J J V V D H N N N A S L A C C L I N
I K A R L B X P E K X G P K D L K Q T O O I T R
V Q D R Y Y V T A C Y B R Q L C P L I M N N I G
E G J E M G S S B R T F E N X E M V V P J K O M
Q R E T C P Y S F N T N D R C D P P E L U I N S
L Z C N V C I K L W U I I D Z Q H K O E N N Q H
W G T I D M O G G O C S C T T R H B S M C G C D
S C I D P P Q M N F N P A I A D J D B E T V X P
W K V L F R C O M R O H T S P E B G G N I E R J
B R E V D A R C L A U S E X C L A M A T O R Y Y
K L C O M P L E X W N C J T B G E L X N N B Z Q
```

| | | |
|---|---|---|
| ADJECTIVE | EXCLAMATORY | OBJECT |
| ADVERB | GERUND | PARTICIPLE |
| CLAUSE | IMPERATIVE | PHRASE |
| COMMA | INFINITIVE | PREDICATE |
| COMPLEMENT | INTERJECTION | PREPOSITION |
| COMPLEX | INTERROGATIVE | PRONOUN |
| COMPOUND | LINKING VERB | SIMPLE |
| CONJUNCTION | NOMINATIVE | SUBJECT |
| DELCARATIVE | NOUN | WORDS |

# 2-27. ADJECTIVES, ADVERBS, AND SPELLING

Good writers use adjectives and adverbs to make their stories and essays more detailed and interesting. Descriptions give the reader a more accurate picture of the character, setting, action, or other facets of the writing. Use strong adjectives and adverbs in your own writing. The benefits will be many.

The letters of the following 20 adjectives and adverbs are in cryptology, meaning these letters are substitutes for the original letters in that word. In this activity, *B* is used for the letter *C* and *N* is used for *R*. Fill in the missing letters in the appropriate spaces. Then, on the back of this sheet, write ten sentences—five using adjectives and five using adverbs found in this cryptology.

1. BYXGN      = _ _ _ _ _ _
2. HNVQXM     = _ _ _ _ _ _ _
3. MVU        = _ _ _
4. CNXKKR     = _ _ _ _ _ _ _
5. LVVM       = _ _ _ _
6. HFXNBXYR   = _ _ _ _ _ _ _ _
7. UXYY       = _ _ _ _
8. NFPFW      = _ _ _ _ _
9. NGNXYR     = _ _ _ _ _ _
10. VMYR      = _ _ _ _
11. BGNXHZYYR = _ _ _ _ _ _ _ _ _
12. LUFHKYR   = _ _ _ _ _ _ _
13. UIXMXAXN  = _ _ _ _ _ _ _ _
14. NVEZLK    = _ _ _ _ _ _
15. LYVUYR    = _ _ _ _ _ _
16. CVUXNHZYYR = _ _ _ _ _ _ _ _ _ _
17. GLKZKX    = _ _ _ _ _ _
18. EXKKXN    = _ _ _ _ _ _
19. TZLBZYGN  = _ _ _ _ _ _ _ _
20. KGYY      = _ _ _ _

## *Letter Identification Code*

| A | B | C | D | E | F | G | H | I | J | K | L | M | N | O | P | Q | R | S | T | U | V | W | X | Y | Z |
|---|---|---|---|---|---|---|---|---|---|---|---|---|---|---|---|---|---|---|---|---|---|---|---|---|---|
| _ | E | B | _ | _ | _ | _ | I | _ | D | _ | _ | T | _ | _ | _ | _ | N | _ | _ | _ | A | _ | O | _ | _ |

# 2-28. PARTS-OF-SPEECH FILL-INS

Knowing these 12 parts of speech will certainly help you do well here. Fill in an appropriate word for the required part of speech. The abbreviations for the parts of speech are given.

| | |
|---|---|
| adj = adjective | n = noun |
| advb = adverb | prep = preposition |
| art = article | pro = pronoun |
| con = conjunction | pro/adj = pronoun that is also an adjective |
| hv = helping verb | sub con = subordinating conjunction |
| mv = main verb | v = verb |

1. _____ _____ _____ _____ _____.
      n               v            prep          art          n

2. _____ _____ _____ _____ _____.
     pro         advb         v         prep        pro

3. _____ _____ _____ _____ _____ _____?
     hv         pro        mv       prep     pro/adj    noun

4. _____ _____ _____ _____?
     hv           pro          mv        advb

5. _____ _____ _____ _____ _____ _____ _____.
     pro     con      pro      hv      mv    pro/adj   advb

6. _____ _____ _____ _____.
     v           art          n       advb

7. _____ _____ _____ _____, _____ _____ _____.
  subcon     n      v      adj     pro    hv     v

8. _____ _____ _____ _____ _____ _____ _____ _____.
    pro    conj    pro     hv     mv   sub con   pro    v

# 2-29. WORKING YOUR WAY THROUGH THE PARTS OF SPEECH

Each sentence below has specific requirements. On the line below the requirements, write a sentence that fulfills the required parts of speech. Remember that a word like *your* or *our* is a pronoun/adjective and the words, *a*, *an*, and *the* are articles. An example sentence has been done for you.

Plural noun—verb—adjective—plural noun—preposition—pronoun/adjective—noun.

<u>Companies showed new products to their stockholders.</u>

1. Pronoun/adjective—noun—verb—article—noun

   _____

2. Pronoun—verb—adjective—conjunction—adjective.

   _____

3. Plural pronoun—verb—adjective—preposition—pronoun/adjective—adjective—noun.

   _____

4. Pronoun—helping verb—main verb—article—adjective—noun.

   _____

5. Pronoun—helping verb—main verb—adverb.

   _____

6. Subordinating conjunction—masculine pronoun—verb,—plural pronoun—verb—pronoun/adjective—plural noun.

   _____

7. Pronoun—verb—preposition—article—adjective—noun.

   _____

8. Article—noun—verb—adjective—noun—preposition—article—pronoun/adjective—noun.

   _____

9. Conjunction—article—feminine noun—conjunction—article—plural noun—verb—pronoun/adjective—noun.

   _____

10. Adverb—conjunction—adverb,—proper noun—verb—article—adjective—noun.

    _____

© 1999 by The Center for Applied Research in Education

# 2-30. MORE PARTS-OF-SPEECH FILL-INS

Fill in the blanks within these 10 sentences with the required part of speech found below the blank. Share your sentences with your classmates.

1. People are _____ about _____ _____.
                 verb              adjective     plural noun

2. I used to _____ a friend _____ _____ music with me.
            verb           pronoun     verb

3. When he was a _____ _____ in the city, she would _____ in the streets.
            adjective     noun              verb

4. When _____ see _____, you will _____ forget the moment.
          pronoun      pronoun       adverb

5. Parents have _____ that they _____ _____.
            verb           verb       adverb

6. _____ _____ _____ will go there now.
      pronoun      conjunction     proper noun

7. Gregory _____ wanted to go _____ them.
           adverb         preposition

8. _____ she _____ I will take _____ advice.
     conjunction       conjunction       adjective

9. This is the _____, my only _____.
          noun          noun

10. _____ _____ _____, _____.
      verb       pronoun       adverb     proper noun

# 2-31. MATCH THE SENTENCE WITH ITS DESCRIPTION

Match the sentences in Group Two with their descriptions in Group One by writing the correct letter in the space next to the description. The punctuation in the Group One descriptions has been purposely omitted. Insert the necessary punctuation.

## Group One

1. ___ adverbial clause—article—plural noun—verb—preposition—pronoun.

2. ___ article—noun—conjunction—article—noun—verb—adverb—preposition—article—adjective—noun.

3. ___ pronoun—verb—conjunction—pronoun—verb.

4. ___ article—adjective—noun—verb—infinitive phrase.

5. ___ participial phrase—article—adjective—noun—verb—pronoun/adjective—noun—conjunction—verb—article—noun—preposition—noun.

6. ___ pronoun—helping verb—adverb—main verb—article—relative pronoun—verb—pronoun.

7. ___ proper noun—conjunction—proper noun—verb—conjunction—verb—prepositional phrase.

8. ___ gerund phrase—verb—adjective.

9. ___ helping verb—article—noun—main verb—article—noun?

10. ___ article—adjective—noun—verb—adverb.

## Group Two

A. She swam and he fished.

B. The unusual jury voted again.

C. Reminded by his mother, the young boy cleaned his room and washed the car before noon.

D. Maddie and Molly ran and sunbathed at the beach.

E. Hiking up the steep mountain was fun.

F. The firemen and the officers walked slowly toward the large window.

G. The entire class wanted to break for recess.

H. They will never see the man who said that.

I. Will the minister address the congregation?

J. After the horses escaped from the barn, the men ran after them.

© 1999 by The Center for Applied Research in Education

# 2-32. DISSECTING THE SENTENCE

*Because Helen and her husband, Richard, own some prized antiques, she constantly receives calls from people who want to purchase these treasures.*

Each of the 22 words in this sentence is an answer to a clue in the crossword puzzle. Each word is only used once.

**ACROSS**

1. one of three pronoun/adjectives
2. another pronoun/adjective
3. adjective found in the adverbial clause
4. main verb of the independent clause
7. relative pronoun
8. pronoun/adjective
9. verb in the infinitive phrase
13. main verb of the adverbial clause
14. feminine singular noun
15. initial word of the infinitive phrase
16. subordinating conjunction

**DOWN**

1. subject of the independent clause
2. last word of the infinitive phrase
3. object of the preposition
4. an appositive
5. direct object in the independent clause
6. preposition
7. verb of the second dependent clause
8. antecedent of Richard
10. adverb
11. direct object in the initial dependent clause
12. conjunction

# SECTION THREE
# SENTENCE ESSENTIALS

# 2-33. FINDING THE 21 VERB PHRASES

Circle the 21 verb phrases in this word-find puzzle. Then, on the other side of this sheet, write ten sentences, each containing one of the phrases contained in this puzzle. The phrases are placed backward, forward, diagonally, and vertically.

```
X Y W H R R H L R W X X A S J C Z S Y J C C M M
W B A M A T M L W B I R P F H B N H X O C B X P
M I S E M S C H Q O E L A V K O D A U P N Q Y T
A N L E V A R T T S U M L Y C O U L D M A K E D
Y F I L X A T I E N T L R D S Q D L J F S Y E D
B J S R W D H L D R I R D E E H J R D D C N Q N
E W T N N O E S Y D A A E H A L W U C J O J I Q
G D E M F C R I E C E Q P V A O I N D I U D S M
O Z N R T Q N K D O B N E T R V D V T P B M O M
I P I I E G Q I J W D W Y H H V E A E J T B P D
N S N G T H D W F S O H T K X G C K K R Y R E X
G G G Q M F O L V N Q N R G Q A I Z N M B N N H
X P Q Z V P F L S L A V K K V C Z M D O L Q I J
S X R D J M V B D C T T J E D N M T D N W W N B
P L D D N K G V R I S R V S K C C D N Z B N G C
F Q N M J R T G T C N A G P F R M R Q Q D X C M
W R B F K Y M Q V D H G C P G N G X M D J B G T
```

AM TRYING
ARE SELECTING
CAN THROW
COULD HAVE WON
COULD MAKE
DID CARRY
DOES HAVE
DO SEE
HAS RIDDEN
HAVE VACATIONED
IS OPENING

MAY BE GOING
MIGHT PAINT
MUST TRAVEL
SHALL RUN
SHOULD JUMP
WAS LISTENING
WERE HOLDING
WILL DELIVER
WILL WORK
WOULD HAVE KNOWN

# 2-34. PLACING THE PREPOSITIONAL PHRASES

Here are 15 prepositional phrases that need a home. Read the sentences below and decide where would be the best place to insert each phrase. Place that phrase's letter on the appropriate line within the sentence. Use each phrase only once. Discuss your answers with your classmates.

| | |
|---|---|
| (A) aboard the ship | (I) like a bird |
| (B) against all odds | (J) of the stock car race |
| (C) at the music concert | (K) on my sister's report card |
| (D) beyond the parking lot | (L) throughout the clouds |
| (E) during the television program | (M) until payday |
| (F) except for Jeremy | (N) within my heart |
| (G) from my aunt | (O) without my father's help |
| (H) in the red dress | |

1. The news _____ was reported on the sports program at eleven o'clock.

2. Because of the thick fog, we could not see _____.

3. The love _____ can never be expressed with mere words!

4. All the students _____ will be going to the house building meeting.

5. We spotted the whale while we were _____.

6. She is _____ in that she is light on her feet.

7. Our airplane was cruising smoothly _____.

8. I will have to wait _____ before I buy the tickets for the trip.

9. _____, the cancer victim lived for another 30 years.

10. There was so much noise _____ that I could barely hear what the actors were saying.

11. That beautiful woman _____ should be a model.

12. This new CD is a birthday gift _____.

13. I would never have been able to be this successful _____.

14. There were three A's and two B's _____.

15. We met our friends backstage _____.

© 1999 by The Center for Applied Research in Education

# 2-35. LOCATING VERBAL PHRASES

Fifteen verbal phrases are hidden in this short composition. Underline the verbal phrase and then write the correct letter—G for a *gerund* phrase, *I* for an *infinitive phrase*, and *P* for a *participial* phrase—above the phrase. If your answers are correct, you will have located five gerund phrases, five infinitive phrases, and five participial phrases.

Walking back toward her stand near the shoreline, the new lifeguard reflected on the past few minutes. After months of rigorous training and several weeks as a rookie guard, she had made her first rescue. The crowd wanted to make her a heroine for her bravery, but she was a rather humble person and this attention would have made her uncomfortable.

Saving another person's life was certainly something to remember. Though it happened only a short while ago, the young girl, recalling the details, now appreciated what she had accomplished. It happened so fast! Seeing the helpless eight-year-old swimmer was her call to action. The child, disregarding his mother's warnings, had gone out too far. Taken by the current, the youngster needed to regain his composure. He could not. The eighteen-year-old lifeguard, grabbing her line and a life preserver, ran toward the boy. She needed to run swiftly so that she could rescue him before it was too late. Reaching this boy in time was paramount. She was well trained in the techniques of rescuing young bathers. Once, she tried to signal to him. He did not see her. She then decided that she could swim out and hold on to him. In about thirty seconds, she reached him. She clutched the boy, swam toward the beach, and carried him to his sister who was waiting with the others near the shore. Handing her first rescue to his family was a proud moment for this new lifeguard.

© 1999 by The Center for Applied Research in Education

# 2-36. VERBALS VYING FOR VICTORY

The verbals are off to the races. Which verbal—the participle (P), the gerund (G), or the infinitive (I)—will appear most often in these sentences? Underline the verbal phrase in each sentence and then write the corresponding letter on the space next to the question's number. If a sentence does not contain a verbal phrase, write the letter N on the appropriate line. At the bottom of the sheet, write the number of times each verbal appeared within these 15 sentences.

1. _____ To become a better speaker was Louise's goal this year.

2. _____ Living in an apartment with her friends, Kate learned many new lessons.

3. _____ Greg was annoying his classmates with his coughing.

4. _____ Leaving early, the president rushed to his limousine.

5. _____ None of the scientists walked to the observatory last Wednesday.

6. _____ Though you may disagree with me, I want you to think more intensely.

7. _____ She succeeded in the law profession by working diligently.

8. _____ Handing out the flyers at the convention was enjoyable.

9. _____ The boys were handing out the flyers at the convention.

10. _____ Handing out the flyers at the convention, the boys enjoyed themselves.

11. _____ Priscilla's greatest asset is her thinking.

12. _____ The drivers racing down the road were quite reckless.

13. _____ Remembering her friend's birthday, Kendra bought a beautiful bracelet for her.

14. _____ The television show, broadcast in over seventy countries, made television history.

15. _____ To her amazement Jill saw the old man sprinting after his grandchildren.

Participles appeared _____ times.

Gerunds appeared _____ times.

Infinitives appeared _____ times.

© 1999 by The Center for Applied Research in Education

# 2-37. FINDING THE 15 PHRASES

Each of these 15 sentences contains a phrase. If you underline and label these phrases correctly on the line next to the question's number, you will find two gerund (G) phrases, two infinitive (I) phrases, two participial (P) phrases, three appositive (A) phrases, three adjective (ADJ) phrases, and three adverb (ADV) phrases.

1. _____ Refreshing her memory, the attorney asked a brilliant question.

2. _____ Massachusetts, one of the New England States, is very scenic.

3. _____ The mountain could be seen from a distance.

4. _____ Each morning the author writes in her hotel room.

5. _____ Realizing the fatal flaw was quite harmful.

6. _____ The man in the striped shirt is the new mayor.

7. _____ Your favorite player needs to win the final category.

8. _____ Our home in Montana will undergo major renovations this fall.

9. _____ Jesse Jackson, the eloquent speaker, will address the crowd tonight.

10. _____ Do you want to make a deli run, Ken?

11. _____ Hiking this challenging mountain is great exercise.

12. _____ Can you help us after the service?

13. _____ This package from your sister is very fragile.

14. _____ Ashley Hightower, the newest choir member, moved here last week.

15. _____ The commuters pushing the train door were angry.

# 2-38. AN OLYMPIAN EXPERIENCE

Four different types of phrases—verb, participial, gerund, and infinitive—are featured in these 15 sentences. Circle the correct letter choice for the underlined phrase in the sentence and write the letter in the appropriate space. If your answers are correct, the letters will spell out two names that will make this activity's title make sense. Write the 15 letters consecutively in the space at the bottom of this sheet. Then write how the names relate to the activity's title.

1. _____ The driver wanted <u>to find a parking space</u>. **(A)** verb **(B)** infinitive **(C)** gerund

2. _____ <u>Finding a parking spot</u>, the driver was elated. **(A)** participial **(B)** verb **(C)** gerund

3. _____ <u>Finding a parking spot</u> was not easy for the driver. **(Q)** verb **(R)** gerund **(S)** participial

4. _____ The driver, <u>finding a parking spot</u>, was elated. **(A)** verb **(B)** gerund **(C)** participial

5. _____ <u>To move to another town</u> was their goal. **(E)** infinitive **(F)** verb **(G)** gerund

6. _____ <u>Moving to another town</u> was their goal. **(J)** participial **(K)** verb **(L)** gerund

7. _____ They <u>were moving</u> to another town. **(N)** participial **(O)** verb **(P)** infinitive

8. _____ <u>Moving to another town</u>, they were happy. **(L)** gerund **(M)** verb **(N)** participial

9. _____ The family members, <u>moving to another town</u>, were happy. **(A)** participial **(B)** gerund **(C)** verb

10. _____ The family's goal was to try <u>to move to another town</u>. **(L)** gerund **(M)** infinitive **(N)** verb

11. _____ <u>Doing twenty-five laps</u>, Laura won her bet. **(U)** participial **(V)** verb **(W)** gerund

12. _____ <u>Doing twenty-five laps</u> was not easy for Laura. **(L)** verb **(M)** participial **(N)** gerund

13. _____ <u>To do twenty-five laps</u> was difficult for Laura. **(I)** infinitive **(J)** gerund **(K)** participial

14. _____ Laura <u>had completed</u> twenty-five laps. **(A)** infinitive **(B)** participial **(C)** verb

15. _____ Laura, <u>doing the twenty-five laps</u>, won her bet. **(G)** infinitive **(H)** participial **(I)** verb

The letters of the correct answers spell out _____ and

_____. They are related to the activity's title because

_____.

© 1999 by The Center for Applied Research in Education

# 2-39. SHOWING VARIETY WITHIN YOUR SENTENCES

Successful writers use words well. They use words to suit their needs, and their readers are the recipients of this talent. You can do the same with your sentences and have the same effect upon your readers. Following the directives, you will become more aware of the possibilities of constructing sentences. Continue to do the same in your daily writings.

1. Use the dependent clause "Because she was very interested in writing" as a sentence starter.

   _____

2. End your sentence with the dependent clause "because she was very interested in writing."

   _____

3. Use the words "to reach the mountain's summit" as an infinitive phrase that ends your sentence.

   _____

4. Start your sentence with the adverb phrase "in the morning."

   _____

5. Use "in the morning" as an adjective phrase.

   _____

6. Use "leaving his home for the first time" as part of a verb phrase.

   _____

7. Use "Leaving his home for the first time" as a participial phrase.

   _____

8. Use "Leaving his home for the first time" as a gerund phrase.

   _____

9. Use the adjectives "old" and "red" to describe a barn.

   _____

10. Use the same two adjectives—"old" and "red"—but insert them in positions different from sentence 9.

   _____

# 2-40. THE CLAUSE COURSE

The race is on! Which clause will win? Will it be the adjectival, the adverbial, or the noun clause? The subordinate (or dependent) clause in each sentence is underlined. If it is an adjectival clause, write the number 1 in the space before the sentence. If it is an adverbial clause, write the number 2, and if it is a noun clause, write the number 3. Add up you numbers and fill in the information at the bottom of the page.

1. _____ The car that was left in your driveway is Mike's.

2. _____ After he returned from the competition, Hank went straight to bed.

3. _____ He told us that he could not recall his first-grade teacher's name.

4. _____ The announcer decided that the contestant had given the correct answer.

5. _____ How will I know if I am the winner?

6. _____ Mrs. Hundley, who wears very fashionable clothes, is our club's new director.

7. _____ What happened after that is still a big question.

8. _____ Ronald gave the baseball to whoever wanted it.

9. _____ It amused those who had seen it.

10. _____ Unless it fits, do not buy it!

11. _____ Wendy looks as if she knows the answer.

12. _____ Dante, who was an Italian, wrote *The Inferno*.

13. _____ I realize that this is important to you.

14. _____ Romeo is the character who fell in love with Juliet.

15. _____ My father is taller than I.

In first place with _____ points is the _____ clause.

In second place with _____ points is the _____ clause.

In third place with _____ points is the _____ clause.

# 2-41. FINDING THE DEPENDENT OR SUBORDINATE CLAUSES

The 13 dependent or subordinate clauses hidden in this word-find puzzle are placed backward, forward, diagonally, and vertically. Circle all 13 and then join each dependent or subordinate clause with your own independent clause to form a sentence. Write your 13 sentences on the back of this sheet.

```
T D G N H A L W Q X Y K D Y N T P H H F G Q U V
H H E S X S S H V P J P H A D H G S M Z T A N L
A T Z I D T Y T H R L B C F M W U O N H H S T H
T F E L R A C E H T R E T F A N C T V Y A L I Y
W F R H G C C Q G O H K H Y L Z R H F S T O L Y
A M E G M B Y W B S U Y M E Q L N A B R S N I T
S B S L R N Y B R F M G S R M Q H T K N T G H Y
G S S X E G K E A K X S H V X E H I S Z A A E C
I G F F K H V M N B T Q W H X Y V C B R N S A G
V F P P F E E H M H H Q W Z E L F A T T D T R V
E D D W N K Y C E W Q H T S M K R N G V S H F H
N D Q E B V Q Y N F G M T G W K N S K O T E R W
T B H Z Y V S N X I J J R E S L W E P R H Y O Z
O W C F M A V P N S S N P B L R V E W H E W M W
U N Z W Y H L L T P P F C B C I G I D M R A Y M
S V N S D T W P V H Y G W N G K H T P D E N O L
O D O T T N A W U O Y T A H W M X W X D X T U Z
```

AFTER THE CAR LEFT
AS LONG AS THEY WANT
AS THOUGH HE KNEW ME
SINCE HE LEFT
SO THAT I CAN SEE IT
THAT STANDS THERE
THAT WAS GIVEN TO US

UNLESS THEY SAY SO
UNTIL I HEAR FROM YOU
WHAT YOU WANT TO DO
WHENEVER SHE CAN
WHILE THE BABY CRIED
WHO GAVE ME HELP

# 2-42. MAKING TWO INTO ONE

The first part of the sentence is found in Group One. The second part is found in Group Two. Match the 2 parts and write the correct 3-letter answer on the line next to the corresponding part in Group One. If your answers are correct, the consecutive letters will spell out a quote from Karen Sunde about a common emotion. Write the full quote on the lines at the bottom of the page.

## Group One

1. _____ If the tire looks flat,

2. _____ Whenever you need help,

3. _____ Because the animal had escaped from the zoo,

4. _____ Since the flag had been frayed by the wind,

5. _____ While the band members were getting ready to go on stage,

6. _____ The school board members were concerned

7. _____ Even though the children struggled to finish their assignment on time,

8. _____ Nostalgia was the feeling

9. _____ The stray dog was spotted

10. _____ Rather than take the bus to school

11. _____ Her smile broadened

## Group Two

CEI. the audience members were trying to find their seats.
EOF. running down the street towards the intersection.
GLI. the teacher would not extend the period to allow them to finish.
HEA. the children were driven by their parents each morning.
IST. there was much fear running through the town.
MPS. that many of the class reunion attendees had that night last spring.
ORE. the committee decided to replace it.
OVE. call us no matter what time of day or night.
TOL. fill it up at the service station.
VEA. when they saw the most recent test scores.
VEN. when she saw her cousins arrive at the train station.

_____

_____

# 2-43. WISE WORDS FROM WISE WOMEN

Each of the following 12 quotes from wise women has been broken up. The first part of the quote is in Group One and the second part is in Group Two. Match the two parts of each quote and write the corresponding letter from Group Two on the line next to its other part in Group One. The quote's author is listed after its second part. Discuss these quotes with your classmates.

## Group One

1. _____ It takes a lot of courage

2. _____ It is never too late

3. _____ In spite of everything

4. _____ You can no more win a war

5. _____ The downhill path is easy,

6. _____ There can be no happiness if the things we believe in

7. _____ The best impromptu speeches

8. _____ The end is nothing;

9. _____ Children require guidance and sympathy

10. _____ We cease loving ourselves

11. _____ One can never consent to creep

12. _____ Time is a dressmaker

## Group Two

A. are the ones written well in advance.—Ruth Gordon

B. to be what you might have been.—George Eliot

C. I still believe that people are really good at heart.—Anne Frank

D. far more than instruction.—Anne Sullivan

E. specializing in alterations.—Faith Baldwin

F. to show your dreams to someone else.—Erma Bombeck

G. the road is all.—Willa Cather

H. if no one loves us.—Mme. De Stael

I. than you can win an earthquake.—Jeannette Rankin

J. but there's no turning back.—Christina Rossetti

K. when one feels an impulse to soar.—Helen Keller

L. are different from the things we do.—Freya Stark

# 2-44. DOUBLE THE SCORE

**Bulletin:** The phrases will win! They will double the combined score of the sentences and the subordinate clauses.

    Now that there are no surprises, here are the game's rules. If a group of words is a phrase, write P on the line next to the question's number. If the words form a subordinate clause, write SC. If the words are a sentence, write S. The question's number constitutes its point value. Total the value of the sentences and subordinate clauses combined. Total the value of the phrases. If your answers are correct, the phrases' value doubles that of the sentences and subordinate clauses combined. Use the spaces at the bottom of this page for your addition. Capital letters and periods have been purposely omitted.

1. _____ to the first class session

2. _____ past the hour

3. _____ practicing her golf game

4. _____ paddling the boat

5. _____ at the start of the race

6. _____ as the bus left the parking lot

7. _____ he did not want to carry the heavy bundle

8. _____ they were all listening to the coach's instructions

9. _____ while we had watched the cartoon

10. _____ settle the argument immediately

11. _____ to help unpack the groceries

12. _____ about the frogs

13. _____ was calling her sister

14. _____ from the barn

15. _____ having a mind of her own

Sentences: _____ Total: _____

Subordinate Clauses: _____ Total: _____

Combined Total of these two: _____

Phrases: _____ Total: _____

# 2-45. DEVELOPING A STORY THROUGH PHRASES

Include the 15 phrases below in your original story. You may insert them wherever you like. Underline the phrases and give the story a title. Though each phrase is in lower-case letters, you may use any of them as sentence starters. Be prepared to explain your decisions. Share your story with your classmates. (Use the back of this sheet to continue your story.)

**Gerund Phrases**
traveling to the store
reaching her goal

**Infinitive Phrases**
to see her cousins
to earn enough money

**Participial Phrases**
walking around the mall
seeing her former boyfriend

**Verb Phrases**
was spending her money
is talking to the waitress
were looking at the merchandise

**Appositive Phrases**
the clerk at the counter
a great bargain

**Adjective Phrases**
with the high-heeled shoes
in the magazine

**Adverb Phrases**
in the morning
without her sister

_____
_____
_____
_____
_____
_____
_____
_____
_____
_____
_____

# 2-46. FILLING IN THE FRAGMENTS

Each of the following groups of words is a fragment. First make each fragment a complete sentence with your own words. Then add the requirement given to you within the parentheses. Underline the requirement in your new sentence. An example is done for you.

> **Example:** Running toward the crowd. (*add a prepositional phrase*)
> Mike was running toward the crowd <u>at the beach</u>.

1. near the stream by the school (*add a participial phrase*)

   _____

2. the mansion that was purchased by the Hammond family (*add a dependent clause*)

   _____

3. wondering what had happened to the other kids (*add a compound subject*)

   _____

4. without a dime to his name (*add an appositive*)

   _____

5. to go to the store by herself (*add an adverb*)

   _____

6. never thinking it would come down to this moment (*add an adjective*)

   _____

7. because most of the people did not want it (*add a gerund phrase*)

   _____

8. its limbs broken (*add a dependent clause*)

   _____

9. just beyond the city limits (*add two adjectives*)

   _____

10. saw his old friends by the movie theater (*add a participial phrase*)

    _____

# 2-47. ADD TO, TAKE FROM, OR MAKE ANOTHER CHANGE

This activity is no picnic! Each group of words is either a fragment or a run-on. Your job is to correct these incomplete or inaccurate groups of words. Write the amended version on the line below the original.

1. near the mouth of the river

   _____

2. he will not be a participant in this contest, he hurt his foot last month

   _____

3. there he is running down the road, you will not catch him now

   _____

4. even though there are over ten days left before the contest ends

   _____

5. during the final days of the Korean War in the early part of the 1950s

   _____

6. bring your books back home and then

   _____

7. Kaneesha and her two friends going to the museum

   _____

8. deciding that this road might be the quicker route to the farm

   _____

9. before all the guests had arrived at the wedding reception

   _____

10. to tow that old car all the way home last night

    _____

11. I cannot go with you, my term paper is not yet finished

    _____

12. she poured the coffee for the customers, then she took their orders

    _____

13. the World Cup is always exciting, the fans really get into it

    _____

14. Kenny, citing the reasons for his improved health

    _____

15. both said that the cab driver drove right by them, he pretended not to see the women

    _____

# 2-48. JIVE WITH FIVE

Knowing the differences between sentences, fragments, and run-ons is essential in this activity. Below are five sentences (S), five fragments (F), and five run-ons (RO). The first word in each question is intentionally left in the lower case. The end punctuation is also deleted. In the space provided, write the letter corresponding to the correct group of words.

1. _____ the children watching the Fourth of July parade were excited

2. _____ near the town's float

3. _____ nothing in the world

4. _____ he was walking by himself, he was lonely

5. _____ beyond the horizon

6. _____ last year all the counties voted for this proposition

7. _____ receiving quite a bit of applause

8. _____ none of these questions appeared on our examination

9. _____ many people watch their calories, they do not want to gain weight

10. _____ turn out the light, it is too bright in here

11. _____ in the early part of the day Joseph walked his two dogs

12. _____ some of the motorcycles were sold, all were very expensive

13. _____ whether or not the groups want to attend the function

14. _____ if they want to practice tomorrow night, please call me

15. _____ allow her to get to see the singer backstage, she thinks he is great

© 1999 by The Center for Applied Research in Education

# 2-49. KNOWING WHEN A GROUP OF WORDS IS A SENTENCE

A *sentence* (S) is a group of words that expresses a complete thought. It has a subject, a verb, and a complete thought. A *fragment* (F) is part of a sentence. It does not express a complete thought. A *run-on* (RO) is two or more sentences improperly joined as one. A run-on generally has one sentence that "runs" into the other sentence.

Within the 15 groups of words below are five sentences, five fragments, and five run-ons. Place the correct abbreviation on the line next to each question's number. The question number constitutes its point value. If your answers are correct, the total of the numbers for the sentences and the fragments are both 44. The run-ons total 32. Since the first answer is *S*, the sentence has 1 point. Find the remaining 119 points!

1. __S__ Because they work so well together, we will assign them the case.

2. _____ Please turn off the light, it is too bright in here.

3. _____ On the same afternoon as the job interview.

4. _____ The car was coming out of the parking lot, we did not see it.

5. _____ Terry writing quite neatly in her notebook.

6. _____ Some of the newspapers reported the incident, they said it was disastrous.

7. _____ One of the most gifted writers of the century.

8. _____ Perhaps you would be better if you drove more slowly.

9. _____ Usually the food here is quite good, today, though, is another story.

10. _____ Ideally, we would like you to return the portfolio by next Thursday.

11. _____ Listen to the brook babbling it is so relaxing.

12. _____ Everybody has the right to decline if that is the case.

13. _____ Accurate instructions are needed.

14. _____ Playing the part of the recluse.

15. _____ Trying to fit the puzzle's pieces in the biggest case in the state's history.

# 2-50. RUNNING DOWN THE RUN-ON SENTENCE

Each of these 15 groups of words is a run-on. Using either a semicolon, a comma and a conjunction, or a period and a capital letter, illustrate how you would correct the run-on. You may delete words as long as the main ideas remain. Be sure to vary the ways in which you correct the run-on problem.

1. We were startled by the crash outside our house we ran out to see what had happened.

2. Eric Clapton is one of the world's best guitar players, he played with the Yardbirds, Cream, and Derek and The Dominoes.

3. A car was sitting on the road's shoulder, for the next two hours the car's driver sat waiting for help.

4. There is no need to hurry we have plenty of time to spare.

5. See if they have given the correct information, if they have not, tell them what to write.

6. There are many important lessons that Mr. Wardell taught me, responsibility is one of them.

7. You cannot do it all by yourself you will need another's help.

8. Paul walked slowly toward his aunt, she reminded me of my own aunt.

9. Canada is a large country it is located north of the United States.

10. He passed me early in the race, then I passed him near the finish line.

11. The cartoon was pretty funny it made my younger sister laugh hysterically.

12. Dry ice is deceptive it can hurt your hands.

13. Please turn out the light, it is too bright in here.

14. We were anticipating the return of our favorite television program we were disappointed that it had been canceled.

15. Jessica's ballet slippers hung on her bedroom wall they brought back good memories for her.

# 2-51. WHERE DID THE OTHER WORDS GO?

Unfortunately, each sentence below is missing words. Fortunately, the remaining words are listed in their original order. On the space below each group of words, fill in words that will make the fragment a complete sentence. The number of words you fill in is up to you. Reread your insertions to make sure you have constructed a complete sentence. An example is done for you.

**Example:** Phil immediately movie
Phil went home immediately after the movie.

1. He wallet couch

   _____

2. Dog barked day

   _____

3. Our repaired times year

   _____

4. Bring papers desk

   _____

5. The tied after quarters

   _____

6. My I turned cover saw

   _____

7. Ants found spilled

   _____

8. A carpenter beautiful shelves

   _____

9. His new spacious

   _____

10. Leave blanket big

   _____

11. His was soothing

   _____

12. Will arrive do?

   _____

13. See if has delivered

   _____

14. Nobody outstanding

   _____

15. It now or

   _____

# IMPROVING
# YOUR SENTENCES

# 2-52. TOO MANY WORDS

As a writer, you strive to be as concise and exact as possible. When you repeat words unnecessarily or use unnecessary words, the reader becomes confused and your ideas lose their power. Good writers do not want to waste words.

In the space provided following each sentence, revise the sentence by eliminating unnecessary words. Make each sentence more concise while still keeping the essential elements of the sentence.

1. All the musicians in this orchestra they play beautiful music.

   _____

   _____

2. Each and every one of the violinists studied many years.

   _____

   _____

3. These men and women who are experienced in their music field are skilled musicians.

   _____

   _____

4. There are seventy people in this orchestra.

   _____

   _____

5. Their musical sounds were audible to our ears.

   _____

   _____

6. At the present time my friend is studying to try to become a musician.

   _____

   _____

7. The members of the high school orchestra are more older than we are.

   _____

   _____

8. In the event that Shane becomes a musician with fame, we will celebrate that occasion of joy.

   _____

   _____

9. Mrs. Harvey, the school's teacher of music, has given Shane her praise on many occasions.

   _____

   _____

10. In as much as Shane, the musician who is talented, and has worked with diligence and perseverance, he might eventually become a member of the orchestra known as the Boston Pops.

   _____

   _____

# 2-53. KEEP IT SIMPLE

The 10 sentences below are too complicated. Each can be simplified. In doing so, you will be composing more concise and effective sentences. The reader will be more interested in what you have to say since he or she will not have to struggle through superfluous words.

On the lines below each wordy sentence, write a more concise sentence that still retains the important information of the original sentence.

1. The woman who is intelligent called her daughter on the telephone.

_____

_____

2. Harry was both laughing and holding his stomach.

_____

_____

3. You should employ common sense when you are in a dangerous situation.

_____

_____

4. Between noon and six o'clock in the evening, Turk enjoys biking and hiking.

_____

_____

5. If possible, I would like you to please send an application for admission to your college.

_____

_____

6. Some of the members of the orchestra in my school intend to go to Canada on the class trip.

_____

_____

7. The blouse that Mary is currently wearing had been purchased by her last August.

_____

_____

8. The car that my father uses to go back and forth to the train station was given to him by Uncle Jerry.

_____

_____

9. The building, the one that was constructed in 1939, was repainted by the Youth Corps.

_____

_____

10. The shoes that you are currently wearing had been your older brother's shoes in the past.

_____

_____

# 2-54. WORDINESS IS OUT

Writers need to be concise. Superfluous words and phrases interrupt the flow of the piece and distract the reader. Thus, empty phrases, inflated phrases, redundancies, and unnecessary repetition of words should be avoided for clarity's sake. Why say ". . . due to the fact that . . ." when the word **because** achieves the same purpose?

Eliminate the wordiness in the following sentences and write a more concise and effective sentence on the line below.

1. At the present time we have no immediate plans.
   _____
   _____

2. For all intents and purposes he would not fit in here.
   _____
   _____

3. When it is all said and done, Judy can do it due to the fact that she is a talented musician.
   _____
   _____

4. By virtue of the fact that Hector is strong, he can lift that heavy rock by himself.
   _____
   _____

5. Regina will be the new clarinet player as far as I'm concerned.
   _____
   _____

6. Keep your hands inside the car at all times.
   _____
   _____

7. There is a statement that just came from the president's office.
   _____
   _____

8. The movie that was the hit of the recent film festival was a comedy by Hank Smith.
   _____
   _____

9. She is the type of person who loves to attract attention.
   _____
   _____

10. Teenagers between thirteen and nineteen need to complete this form in order to be able to vote in the election next year.
    _____
    _____

11. In a manner of speaking, the procedure of transplanting an organ is a feat of amazement to me.
    _____
    _____

12. In my opinion, the game can be won with the utilization of the field goal, more or less.
    _____
    _____

# 2-55. LET'S NOT OVERSTATE IT

Good writers believe in the expression "Say it without hitting the reader over the head with it." There are many ways to write that someone is unhappy. For instance, the effective writer allows the reader to know that Mark is unhappy by writing "Mark cried privately when he learned that he did not make the soccer team." If the sentence read "Mark was unhappy and he cried privately because he did not make the soccer team," the reader would "be hit over the head" with the author's intentions. Why say the word *unhappy?* It is redundant. Be precise and be concise. Do not overstate the case.

Twelve moods are listed below. For each mood, write an illustrative sentence that clearly indicates that particular mood. You might want to read your sentences to a classmate to see if he or she can identify the mood you have illustrated.

1. concern _____
   _____

2. happiness _____
   _____

3. ecstasy _____
   _____

4. frustration _____
   _____

5. fatigue _____
   _____

6. uncertainty _____
   _____

7. poise _____
   _____

8. anger _____
   _____

9. fright _____
   _____

10. loneliness _____
    _____

11. embarrassment _____
    _____

12. conceit _____
    _____

# 2-56. ONE'S RIGHT AND ONE'S WRONG

Each pair of sentences has one sentence that contains no mistakes. Circle the letter of the correctly written sentence. Then correct the mistake(s) in the incorrectly written sentence. There might be more than one mistake in an incorrectly written sentence. If your answers are correct, the letters of the correctly written sentences will spell out a 10-letter word that is the first word of both a famous building and a firearm.

1. **(T)** Their is more then one way to due this.

   **(W)** Even if you are older, you are not always right.

2. **(O)** Both brothers are taller than me.

   **(I)** Each of the twelve contestants receives some prize.

3. **(D)** Me and my brother will be going with you.

   **(N)** Neither the girls nor their brother has the safe's combination.

4. **(C)** Remember me.

   **(E)** Stopping by woods on a snowy evening.

5. **(I)** He went to the store, and bought a pair of pants.

   **(H)** He bought a pair of pants, and she bought a pair of stockings.

6. **(S)** Its the principal of the thing that bothers me.

   **(E)** You're on the mark with your assessment of the situation.

7. **(S)** Michael, along with his fraternity brothers, drives to the event each year.

   **(O)** He enjoys bowling, biking, and visits to his grandmother.

8. **(W)** They divided the candy between the four children.

   **(T)** Most of the balloons had burst by then.

9. **(N)** There correct in saying that.

   **(E)** This year we read "The Black Cat" and <u>To Kill a Mockingbird</u>.

10. **(E)** Because he was going away on vacation.

    **(R)** The class members enjoy playing intramurals each Friday afternoon.

# 2-57. THE 49'ERS

First, number the words in each of these 10 sentences. Thus for Group One's first sentence, place a small number 1 above the word *After*, a small number 2 above the word *she*, and so forth. Insert the commas wherever they belong within these sentences.

Then, after each sentence, write the number(s) of the word(s) that have commas following them. There may be more than one word for each sentence. Add up the totals for each group. If this is done correctly, the combined total of groups One and Three is 49. The combined total for groups Two and Four is also 49. Check to see you have inserted the commas correctly.

## Group One

1. After she left the pool area she went back to her hotel room.

2. Our class president Marti Challie will be traveling to Nashua New Hampshire.

## Group Two

1. Are you going bowling with us tonight Pauline?

2. The group had always loved to bowl to ski and to jog.

## Group Three

1. To tell you the truth I think you will enjoy yourselves more if you go to Europe during the cooler fall months.

2. If you think that it is wiser to go by train you should do so.

3. Cindy has studied math science and social studies.

## Group Four

1. Whether you arrive early or late we need to get together at some time that night.

2. Have you tried calling his room Mrs. Bernhard?

3. Beautiful Moepuffs our favorite female artist is fantastic!

4. We have never lived in Atlanta Georgia.

# 2-58. DETECTING SENTENCE ERRORS

Four types of sentence errors are found in the sentences below. Write the error's corresponding number on the appropriate line and then correct the error either within/adjacent to the sentence or on the reverse side of this paper.

The four types of errors are **(1)** misplaced or dangling modifier, **(2)** subject-verb agreement, **(3)** pronoun usage, and **(4)** verb form. The number **(5)** indicates a sentence that contains no errors. If your answers are correct, each number appears four times. Each number's total equals 42. The question number constitutes its point value. Thus, since **5** is the answer to the first question, **5** earns one point. See that each number earns 42 points!

1. __5__ Some of the bread loaf is missing.

2. _____ I had ate enough to satisfy two people.

3. _____ Me and he are going swimming in the lake.

4. _____ The oysters in the ocean is beautiful.

5. _____ Washing the dishes, the phone rang.

6. _____ We saw the flowers walking to school yesterday.

7. _____ Peanut butter and jelly are my favorite kind of sandwich.

8. _____ I am taller than him.

9. _____ We could of won the game.

10. _____ The taller they are, the harder they fall.

11. _____ Because Frank is so popular, the students voted him their class president.

12. _____ We had swam in the Atlantic two years ago.

13. _____ The gift was given to Gina and I.

14. _____ Neither the girls nor their brother were going to the airport.

15. _____ To become a good baseball pitcher, the ball must be thrown with speed and accuracy.

16. _____ Hurrying to the meeting, the woman's portfolio was dropped in the hallway.

17. _____ One of the mechanics are going on vacation next week.

18. _____ The group members did the entire project by theirselves.

19. _____ We found that the dryer had shrank the shirt.

20. _____ Due to budgetary concerns, the company moved to another state.

© 1999 by The Center for Applied Research in Education

# 2-59. CUTTING OUT THE CONFUSION

Twenty-nine words that are often confused provide the clues in this crossword puzzle. Write the word that is often confused with the clue word. Thus, since *capitol* is the clue for #1 Across, the answer is *capital*, the word commonly confused with its clue word. Good luck!

**ACROSS**

1. capitol
6. counsel
8. alter
10. dessert
11. quite
14. except
16. here
17. piece
19. week
22. shown
23. through
24. whether

**DOWN**

1. site
2. their
3. led
4. too
5. loose
6. course
7. compliment
8. effect
9. break
12. than
13. principle
14. advise
15. past
17. plane
18. clothes
20. formerly
21. stationery

© 1999 by The Center for Applied Research in Education

# 2-60. AVOIDING THE PASSIVE VOICE

In most instances, writers prefer to use the **active voice**. In the sentence "Larry walked his dog," **Larry** is the subject, the one who acts. If written using the **passive voice**, the sentence would read, "The dog was walked by his owner, Larry." Here the subject, **dog**, is acted upon. The doer, **Larry**, is obscured by the sentence's construction, namely, the passive voice choice. Thus, for both emphasis and clarity, the active voice is preferred over the passive voice. Though there are some occasions when the passive voice should be used ("The house was struck by lightning."), your sentences will generally flow more naturally when you use the active voice.

Change these 12 sentences from the passive voice to the active voice. Remember to use the active voice in your writing.

1. The packages were carried to the car by Jaime and Jaylen.

   _____

2. The starring roles in **Pygmalion** were played by Thomas and Gertrude.

   _____

3. After the snowstorm the roads were plowed by the crew.

   _____

4. The students were asked by the teacher if they wanted to take a break.

   _____

5. There were at least one hundred people standing on line.

   _____

6. It was thrilling for the parents to hear the great news about their son.

   _____

7. There were three reasons why she was not elected to the position.

   _____

8. In the summer many surfboards are bought by teenagers.

   _____

9. The room should be cleaned by both of you before you go out tonight.

   _____

10. The signal was given by the director to the cast members.

    _____

11. A corny joke was told to the crowd by the skinny comedian.

    _____

12. There are many ways that Barbara can win his affection.

    _____

# 2-61. ANIMALS IN SIMILES

The literary device called the **simile** is a comparison of 2 seemingly unlike things using the words *like* or *as*. This figure of speech used by the writer appeals to the reader's imagination by painting a picture or conveying an impression.

    Fifteen animals are featured in the similes below. Show you understand each animal's characteristics by completing the similes. Write the correct letter in the appropriate space next to the number.

1. _____ bear

2. _____ beaver

3. _____ bird

4. _____ cheetah

5. _____ elephant

6. _____ fox

7. _____ giraffe

8. _____ lamb

9. _____ lark

10. _____ mule

11. _____ owl

12. _____ ox

13. _____ snail

14. _____ swan

15. _____ tiger

A. as crafty as a(n)

B. as eager as a(n)

C. as ferocious as a(n)

D. as free as a(n)

E. as graceful as a(n)

F. as happy as a(n)

G. as heavy as a(n)

H. as hungry as a(n)

I. as meek as a(n)

J. as slow as a(n)

K. as strong as a(n)

L. as stubborn as a(n)

M. as swift as a(n)

N. as tall as a(n)

O. as wise as a(n)

© 1999 by The Center for Applied Research in Education

# 2-62. KICKING OUT THE CLICHÉS

Clichés are overused expressions that lack originality and freshness. "As fresh as a daisy," "walking on eggs," and "beating around the bush" are used too frequently to be effective in good writing.

Each sentence below contains a cliché. Cross out the cliché and write a more original way of saying the same idea. Share your answers with your classmates.

1. I will be your loyal friend come rain or shine.

   _____

2. After training hard for so many years, Bob was as fit as a fiddle.

   _____

3. Molly's new infant is as light as a feather.

   _____

4. She often found herself behind the eight ball.

   _____

5. The doctor told the heavy drinker that he should go cold turkey.

   _____

6. The story they told us is as old as the hills.

   _____

7. Needless to say, her performance proved that she was under the weather.

   _____

8. Now that your parents have seen your grades, you had better toe the line.

   _____

9. Those merchants are guilty of highway robbery.

   _____

10. Your artistic talent is nothing to sneeze at.

    _____

11. Upon receiving the news, Martin was as happy as a clam.

    _____

12. Watch out! That man is dumb like a fox.

    _____

13. Professor Prescott knows this procedure like the back of his hand.

    _____

14. Those two are like two peas in a pod.

    _____

15. Last weekend it rained cats and dogs on the mainland.

    _____

# 2-63. EXPLAINING THE IDIOMS

An idiom is sometimes referred to as an "untranslatable expression." The words in an idiom cannot be taken literally. As an example, what does it mean "to hear it straight from the horse's mouth"? Did you ever "rub someone the wrong way"? These expressions are idioms.

Here is your chance to explain the unexplainable. Rewrite the original sentence by replacing each idiom with your own words. Use your dictionary if necessary. The first one is done for you.

1. His incessant finger tapping was driving her up the wall.

   His incessant finger tapping was making her crazy. _____

2. Juanita felt that she was between a rock and a hard place.

   _____

   _____

3. It was like finding a needle in a haystack.

   _____

   _____

4. She felt that the only thing she could do was to grin and bear it.

   _____

   _____

5. Unfortunately for the team members, it was time to face the music.

   _____

   _____

6. Both families decided it was best to bury the hatchet.

   _____

   _____

7. Kevin believed our story—hook, line, and sinker.

   _____

   _____

8. After only a few minutes of the contest, I knew I was in over my head.

_____

_____

9. This was my chance to kill two birds with one stone.

_____

_____

10. It was a case of the pot calling the kettle black.

_____

_____

11. Don't you think that you are cutting off your nose to spite your face?

_____

_____

12. Roberta felt that her new job placed her in the catbird's seat.

_____

_____

13. Steven had put his foot in his mouth too many times.

_____

_____

14. The detectives were playing it close to the vest.

_____

_____

15. Keep your ear to the ground.

_____

_____

Write some other clichés you know on the following lines.

_____

_____

_____

_____

# SHAPING SENSATIONAL SENTENCES

# 2-64. THREE-WORD SENTENCES

This activity will test your vocabulary and sentence-building skills. Three different columns—adjective, noun, and verb—are to be filled in with the appropriate words. For each letter in the Letter Column, you must use a word beginning with that letter in each of the spaces. Thus, **Agile acrobats appear** suffices the requirements since all three begin with **a** and they are the required parts of speech. Try your best to construct logical sentences. Some may be humorous! Share them with your classmates.

| Letter Column | Adjective | Noun | Verb |
| --- | --- | --- | --- |
| A | | | |
| B | | | |
| C | | | |
| D | | | |
| E | | | |
| F | | | |
| G | | | |
| H | | | |
| I | | | |
| J | | | |
| K | | | |
| L | | | |
| M | | | |
| N | | | |
| O | | | |
| P | | | |
| Q | | | |
| R | | | |
| S | | | |
| T | | | |
| U | | | |
| V | | | |
| W | | | |
| X | | | |
| Y | | | |
| Z | | | |

# 2-65. SCRAMBLED SENTENCES

The words in the following 12 sentences have been scrambled. Rearrange each sentence's words and write them in the correct order on the lines after the sentence. Use correct punctuation.

1. Did glass shatter the?

   _____

   _____

2. please door you go Before the lock.

   _____

   _____

3. Our for fifteen warm up minutes us to coach told.

   _____

   _____

4. water swimming let's go warm is Since the.

   _____

   _____

5. shop repair in are Both cars the.

   _____

   _____

6. room fan Will entire the cool this?

   _____

   _____

7. The garage is hammock the in.

   _____

   _____

8. and then envelope the Seal it mail.

   _____

   _____

9. movie drama and police officers about is a The work their.

   _____

   _____

10. These CD's bought I ever the are best have new.

    _____

    _____

11. you both The wants firm hire to of.

    _____

    _____

12. We meet game you soccer after your will.

    _____

    _____

© 1999 by The Center for Applied Research in Education

# 2-66. JOINING WORDS TO MAKE SENTENCES

Using the words next to each number below and words of your own choice, construct a sentence. Do not change the form of the words given to you; however, you may change the words' order. Write the sentence on the lines immediately below the words. Compare your answers with those of your classmates.

1. swiftly . . . she . . . track

_____

_____

2. don't . . . again . . . why

_____

_____

3. probably . . . summer . . . I

_____

_____

4. is . . . favorite . . . group

_____

_____

5. three . . . stopped . . . on

_____

_____

6. me . . . what . . . tomorrow

_____

_____

7. unless . . . take . . . critical

_____

_____

8. any . . . might . . . terrific

_____

_____

9. might . . . well . . . must

_____

_____

10. there . . . suggestion . . . wrongdoing

_____

_____

# 2-67. CONSTRUCTING THE SENTENCES

Each of the 12 sentences has been broken up into three parts. The subjects appear in Column A, the verbs are in Column B, and the phrases that complete the sentences are in Column C. Below the three columns, reconstruct the original 12 sentences using the letters assigned to each component. Since each part is used only once, construct the most logical sentences possible. The first one is done for you.

| Column A | Column B | Column C |
|---|---|---|
| (A) The actress | (A) argued | (A) at the state fair. |
| (B) The coach | (B) climbed | (B) for her client. |
| (C) The comb | (C) hit | (C) from the sidelines. |
| (D) The cowboy | (D) ran | (D) into second base. |
| (E) The doctor | (E) rode the horse | (E) into the burning house. |
| (F) The fireman | (F) served | (F) into the hospital ward. |
| (G) The golfer | (G) signaled | (G) into the wind. |
| (H) The lawyer | (H) slid | (H) on the bathroom floor. |
| (I) The lifeguard | (I) walked | (I) to the audience. |
| (J) The policeman | (J) was found | (J) to the oncoming motorist. |
| (K) The runner | (K) waved | (K) toward the poor swimmer. |
| (L) The waitress | (L) yelled | (L) until eleven o'clock. |

A — K — I        E — __ — __        I — __ — __

B — __ — __      F — __ — __        J — __ — __

C — __ — __      G — __ — __        K — __ — __

D — __ — __      H — __ — __        L — __ — __

# 2-68. CONSECUTIVE LETTERS

Consecutive letters are the order of the day. Compose 4-word sentences following the directives given to you. The second, third, and fourth words follow each other alphabetically. Thus, in the first sentence, a possible answer is *An old plumber quit*. You select the articles *a*, *an*, or *the* for the first word of the sentence. After that, you must use the consecutive letters that start the words.

1. An *old* *plumber* *quit*.

2. ____ i_____ j_____ k_____.

3. ____ b_____ c_____ d_____.

4. ____ u_____ v_____ w_____.

5. ____ f_____ g_____ h_____.

6. ____ l_____ m_____ n_____.

7. ____ a_____ b_____ c_____.

8. ____ j_____ k_____ l_____.

9. ____ c_____ d_____ e_____.

10. ____ t_____ u_____ v_____.

11. ____ s_____ t_____ u_____.

12. ____ e_____ f_____ g_____.

13. ____ g_____ h_____ i_____.

14. ____ d_____ e_____ f_____.

15. ____ k_____ l_____ m_____.

16. ____ p_____ q_____ r_____.

17. ____ h_____ i_____ j_____.

18. ____ z_____ a_____ b_____.

19. ____ y_____ z_____ a_____.

20. ____ e_____ f_____ g_____.

# 2-69. THE PROPER ARRANGEMENT

The order of the words in each of the 10 sentences below has been jumbled. Rearrange each sentence's words so that the sentence reads correctly. Write the correct arrangement on the lines below the jumbled version of the sentence. Some of the sentences can be rearranged in more than one way. The correct version's first word has been capitalized for you.

1. served at was o'clock promptly seven Dinner.

   _____

   _____

2. from received groups funds different had They.

   _____

   _____

3. the people stranded storm At least by seventy were.

   _____

   _____

4. could laugh his humorous The easily make teachers student.

   _____

   _____

5. economy is declining challenging Dealing a with.

   _____

   _____

6. bicentennial invited Our officials town's our foreign to dignitaries.

   _____

   _____

7. fast can't build accommodate We to enough rising population the houses.

   _____

   _____

8. Bobby and his colleagues of pay raises for most asked.

   _____

   _____

9. Be clams them eating cook these sure to before.

   _____

   _____

10. for the customers confusing new fees produced charges Hidden.

   _____

   _____

© 1999 by The Center for Applied Research in Education

© 1999 by The Center for Applied Research in Education

# 2-70. CPR FOR THESE SENTENCES!

These 12 sentences need immediate attention! They are dull and lifeless. To say that they are boring might be a compliment. Make these 12 sentences come alive by adding descriptive adverbs and adjectives. Add more specifics. Use more accurate and vivid verbs. Essentially, give them some CPR! Write the improved versions on the lines below the original sentence. An example sentence is offered.

**Example:** The machine broke.
Our ten-year-old car's motor seized on the highway yesterday.

1. A building was damaged.
_____
_____

2. The woman had a reason to be very happy.
_____
_____

3. The people were there.
_____
_____

4. They heard the noise.
_____
_____

5. He saw it then.
_____
_____

6. It was over quickly.
_____
_____

7. He told me to do it.
_____
_____

8. She was there already.
_____
_____

9. Someone found it.
_____
_____

10. A man appeared.
_____
_____

11. It had been a success.
_____
_____

12. The trip was enjoyable for them.
_____
_____

# 2-71. USING MODIFIERS EFFECTIVELY

The sentence "The woman walked toward the stage" is rather bland. Inserting a few modifiers—including adjectives, adverbs, phrases, and clauses—will improve the sentence. The new sentence "The tall, well-dressed woman walked confidently toward the auditorium's large stage" tells much more and adds life to the original idea. This is the essence of effective descriptive writing.

Following the directives given for each base sentence, write the new sentence on the appropriate line.

**Base Sentence:** Jose did the assignment in two hours.

Replace *did* with a better verb: _____

Add an adjective: _____

Add an adverb: _____

**Base Sentence:** The child ran from the dog.

Replace *ran* with a better verb: _____

Add an adjective: _____

Add an adverb: _____

Add a prepositional phrase: _____

**Base Sentence:** The letter carrier walked.

Replace *walked* with a better verb: _____

Add an adjective: _____

Add an adverb: _____

Add a verbal phrase: _____

**Base Sentence:** The program was boring.

Add a prepositional phrase: _____

Add a dependent clause: _____

Add an adverb: _____

**Base sentence:** His sister wrote a screenplay.

Add a participial phrase: _____

Add a dependent clause: _____

Add an appositive: _____

© 1999 by The Center for Applied Research in Education

# 2-72. MATCHING THE DEPENDENTS WITH THE INDEPENDENTS

Match the 10 dependent clauses in Column A with their logical independent clause counterparts in Column B. Write the correct matching letter after the number in Column A. Use each number and letter only once.

## Column A

1. ___ After the rain shower stopped,

2. ___ Although the sun was ferocious,

3. ___ Because she is tall,

4. ___ If you feel you can do all the required work,

5. ___ Once the coach spotted Bob, the soccer player, taking it easy during practice,

6. ___ Since the class will be released early today,

7. ___ Unless they pay the fee,

8. ___ When the opportunity presents itself,

9. ___ Whenever I am feeling lonely,

10. ___ While the dentist examined my teeth,

## Column B

A. both explorers continued their way across the desert.

B. Helen was asked to try out for the basketball team.

C. I go to the mall to see other people.

D. Mrs. Hoffman, the nurse, assisted him.

E. she became angry and made him do extra sprints.

F. the sun came out again.

G. the school officials had to notify the bus company.

H. they will not be allowed to go on the class trip.

I. write to your grandmother who misses you dearly.

J. you should become a member of the honors class.

# 2-73. MATCHING THE CAUSE AND THE EFFECT

Consider the sentence "The driver was late because her bus had broken down on the highway." The cause is "because her bus had broken down on the highway," and the effect is "the driver was late."

The causes and effects of 10 sentences have been placed in two columns. Match the correct cause with its appropriate effect and then write that complete sentence on the lines following the 2 columns. (Use the back of this sheet if you need more space.) Commas, periods, and certain capital letters have been purposely omitted. Since each cause and each effect are used only once, try to match the 10 most logical causes and effects.

| *Causes* | *Effects* |
|---|---|
| because Harrison Ford is such a terrific actor | he could not use his credit card |
| because he reads slowly | he takes a long time to finish a novel |
| because her mom had died last year | his movies are big money-makers |
| because it was raining | Janice has had to take on more responsibility |
| because she has a great sense of humor | she was given a sports scholarship to college |
| because Terry is an outstanding athlete | she was voted Class Clown |
| in order to hear the sound | the band members played longer |
| since it was stolen | we could not go sailing |
| so that they could make more money | we turned up the volume |
| unless you have a ticket | you cannot get into the concert |

_____

_____

_____

_____

_____

_____

# 2-74. ADDING TO THE SENTENCE BASE

You will overhaul 5 simple sentences. For each sentence add more information so that it is more specific and more interesting. Mark the additions in the same way that the additions to the example sentence have been marked.

**Example sentence base:** We purchased the car.
**What to add:** two adjectives, an adverb, a dependent clause

         advb.       adj.  adj.     dep. cl.
**Improved sentence:** We <u>eagerly</u> purchased the <u>black</u>, <u>antique</u> car <u>that the dealer had displayed in the showroom</u>.

1. **Sentence base:** The group was divided.

   **What to add:** an adjective, a prepositional phrase, a dependent clause

   **Improved sentence:** _____

   _____

   _____

2. **Sentence base:** The bicycle was on the car's roof.

   **What to add:** an adverb, a main verb, a dependent clause

   **Improved sentence:** _____

   _____

   _____

3. **Sentence base:** Francine likes to work out in the morning.

   **What to add:** an additional subject, an adverb

   **Improved sentence:** _____

   _____

   _____

4. **Sentence base:** The cat meowed.

   **What to add:** an adverb, an adjective, a prepositional phrase, a dependent clause

   **Improved sentence:** _____

   _____

   _____

5. **Sentence base:** My brother cried.

   **What to add:** an adjective, an adverbial clause, an adverb, a prepositional phrase

   **Improved sentence:** _____

   _____

   _____

# 2-75. FOLLOW-UP SENTENCES

Here is your chance to help another writer. She gives you the first sentence of a composition and now needs you to add the next line. Yet, that is only half of what you are asked to do. After you have written the next line on the appropriate space, tell what purpose you hope to attain with that line. Do you want to create suspense? Set a mood? Develop character? Increase intensity? Some other purpose? Be prepared to support your reasons. An example sentence is done for you.

**Example:** I will never forget the first time I saw New York City. <u>The fast-paced crowds, the tall buildings, the street vendors, and the amount of traffic astounded me.</u> (*mood*)

1. We heard a strange sound coming from our basement. _____
   _____

2. It was a day like no other. _____
   _____

3. There comes a time in one's life when all of a sudden things are not as they once were. _____
   _____

4. Why had I said that to him? _____
   _____

5. Last December I realized my life had changed drastically. _____
   _____

6. Exercise is essential for good health. _____
   _____

7. My neighborhood is unique. _____
   _____

8. My alarm failed to ring for the third time this week. _____
   _____

9. The hailstones pelted the roof of our cabin. _____
   _____

10. I would not believe this story had it not happened to me. _____
    _____

11. The police officer's stern look as she approached our car made us feel very uneasy. _____
    _____

12. A group of tough-looking guys had been following me since I came out of the subway station. _____
    _____

# 2-76. DETAILS NEVER HURT

Dull sentences are just that—dull! The sentence that reads "The sky is pretty" does little to help the reader. What details could make this sentence come alive, be more exciting and realistic? "The cloudless sky above the snow-capped mountain was breathtaking" is a better sentence since it is more detailed and exact.

Make the following lifeless sentences come alive by adding more details. Use your dictionary for the best words. Share your sentences with your classmates.

1. The food had a bad taste. _____

_____

2. The inside of the car was dirty. _____

_____

3. The exam was difficult. _____

_____

4. The doctor had bad news. _____

_____

5. Our house looked beautiful. _____

_____

6. The photograph was interesting. _____

_____

7. The book was exciting. _____

_____

8. The discussion was heated. _____

_____

9. The building was big. _____

_____

10. The movie was moving. _____

_____

11. The flowers were pretty. _____

_____

12. Tom felt funny. _____

_____

# WRITING MORE MATURELY

# 2-77. CONNECTING THE WORDS

Below are 25 words that make up three sentences that logically follow one another. Reconstruct these original three sentences and write them on the lines. The words have been placed in a certain order. Find the first word of the original sentence, and then continue along, remembering that only the words in the adjacent boxes (above, below, or next to) can follow directly after. Thus, capital letters have been inserted to help you. The first sentence begins with "Tomorrow morning our . . ."

| will | visit | the | will | we |
| our | group | Museum | travel | Finally |
| morning | Tomorrow | of | home | show |
| Then | History | Natural | Broadway | see |
| we | will | go | to | a |

_____

_____

_____

_____

_____

_____

_____

_____

_____

_____

_____

_____

_____

_____

_____

# 2-78. PUTTING THEM BACK TOGETHER

The words from three sentences are listed alphabetically below. Using all these words, reconstruct the three original sentences. Each sentence contains 7 words. The first sentence begins with the word *Doctor*; the second sentence begins with the word *A*; and the third sentence begins with the word *Her*. Write the three sentences on the lines below.

| A | diagnosed | for | mononucleosis | the |
| as | Doctor | Her | road | the |
| blue | down | is | Samson | tomorrow |
| car | family | leaving | sped | vacation |
| case | | | | |

_____

_____

_____

_____

_____

_____

_____

_____

_____

_____

_____

_____

_____

_____

# 2-79. FOLLOWING A HARDER PATH

The following 25 words have been taken from two sentences. On the lines below, reconstruct the two original sentences so that all 25 words are used. If you find that too difficult, construct sentences of your own so that only these 25 words (and no others) are used. **Hint:** For the original two sentences, the word *He* starts the first sentence and *They* starts the second.

| | | | | |
|---|---|---|---|---|
| and | have | places | that | travel |
| can | He | plans | They | traveled |
| countries | he | schedule | this | various |
| exotic | his | seven | to | work |
| family | his | so | to | year |

_____

_____

_____

_____

_____

_____

_____

_____

_____

_____

_____

_____

_____

_____

_____

_____

_____

_____

# 2-80. FOUR SENTENCES

Four sentences have been broken up and their words have been placed in the categories below. Using all (and only) these words once each, reconstruct the original four sentences. They do not necessarily go in any special order. Write your answers on the appropriate lines.

**adjectives:** elderly; sixteen

**articles (not found in prepositional phrases):** an; the; the

**direct object:** street

**prepositional phrases:** in the fields; in the park; into the emergency room; of cows; of the doctors

**pronoun/adjective:** our

**subjects:** boys; all; herd; woman

**verbs/ verb phrases:** crossed; had grazed; were called; were playing

First sentence: _____

_____

Second sentence: _____

_____

Third sentence: _____

_____

Fourth sentence: _____

_____

Bonus: Write any sentence that has two subjects, two verbs, two conunctions, and two preposi- tional phrases.

_____

_____

# 2-81. TRANSITIONAL WORDS WORD-FIND

Each of these 25 words is used as a transition that joins ideas between or within sentences. In the sentence "Afterward, we ate lunch," the word *afterward* acts as a transition from one sentence to another. Circle the 25 transitional words in this word-find puzzle. The words are are placed backward, forward, diagonally, and vertically.

```
X V L W F B T N W X P B W D N Y Z L J R A S I H
L D Z P G B X L M Z Z F U P P J E Q E L L I N Y
M O R E O V E R O M R E H T R U F T F R S M S D
F F H A W P N S Z P C D H T S S A Y D O O I T M
I N S B W O J S I N L U L H D L W C O G C L E P
N J E Y G R T P E D S L O E Q R S N Q V O A A K
A C Y V Y Q E H O W E V E R M L L N K Z N R D Y
L C L Z E G T T E T B S Q E S J E D T W S L P S
L M C R G R Q B F R W T F F K H P S H R E Y G J
Y I M O C B T Z M A W B F O W C Q I L J Q B T Q
H D K P R R R H S H W I P R S T L G D Q U B S T
M T Y E Y D Z Y E W C C S E F E F T X T E K W Z
W G F M W V I P X L Q N X E Z S B B K F N P C T
F C L X Y I W N W D E Z K Z S T X Q M R T W Y T
P L S B D T S P G W K S T Y G G J Z N D L Z X F
H Y Z H Y K R E V L L H S B D P H C K N Y H C G
Q T B V W C W F H B Y T P W R W J D F C T L H R
```

| ACCORDINGLY | FINALLY | MEANWHILE | SOON |
| --- | --- | --- | --- |
| AFTERWARD | FURTHERMORE | MOREOVER | THEREFORE |
| ALSO | HENCE | NEVERTHELESS | THUS |
| BESIDES | HOWEVER | NEXT | WHEN |
| BUT | INSTEAD | OR | YET |
| CONSEQUENTLY | LATER | OTHERWISE | |
| | LIKEWISE | SIMILARLY | |

# 2-82. SUBORDINATING CONJUNCTIONS WORD FIND

Nineteen dependent clauses are listed below the puzzle. The subordinating conjunctions that start each clause are hidden within the puzzle. Some subordinating conjunctions are one word, some are two, and some are three. Circle the 19 subordinating conjunctions. The words are placed backward, forward, diagonally, and vertically. Good luck!

```
L F D J C R W A H T K J G T S N S P N X Y H Y H
C I Z E R H E D F D J B T N C P N C A F H X P C
Y G T C E W V V J T F F M G A D V B H D H Z N H
W H E N E V E R F K E Z X N S D N Z T Z B F G Y
H H H O U G N N L L C R Q F J X P A R L I U Y C
E I I P W V T W V L N X K H N X H K E N O X S J
R N F L H B H J W W I Q T Y X T C N H H K G H N
E O L B E F O R E X S T T R X E T N T S B W N G
A R T N R R U S V M K X X D S X Q L A R L A L N
S D Q G E C G L M G D T Z U S T A R R K H B G F
K E N K N M H N C H T Z A R G S N S G T R M B P
J R R L M M P K W H X C N M P V S F V Z N K X P
F T J J Y J W L L K E F H P V L V W W S R Z Z K
B H C Z J L L Y C B N Q N H T S F B K V N H M Z
B A Y P S Q R Y Y H Z M Y W H Q Y Q N W M Z V B
P T H M P V Q F P D H L P C Z C J G Q Z B S X K
Z L G L T K K F T G K J P C C X R Q L J H T P L
```

AFTER THE GAME CONCLUDED
ALTHOUGH HE IS TALLER NOW
AS THE RAIN WAS FALLING
BECAUSE THEY WILL HELP YOU
BEFORE THE FLOOD OCCURRED
EVEN THOUGH KYLE IS THE RIGHT CHOICE
IN ORDER THAT EVERYBODY IS HAPPY
ONCE YOU CAN FIND THE SOLUTION
RATHER THAN YOUR SELECTING THE PLAYERS

SINCE I AM THE CAPTAIN OF THIS TEAM
THAN I AM
THAT HE HAS SOLD YOU
TILL YOU SEE THEM AGAIN
UNTIL THE CAR WAS BROUGHT TO THE NEXT STATION
WHEN THE LAST SLIDE WAS VIEWED
WHENEVER I FEEL LONELY
WHERE THE TWO ROADS MEET
WHEREAS SHE WILL VOUCH FOR YOU
WHILE THE PARADE PASSES BY

# 2-83. CRYPTIC CONJUNCTIONS

The letters of 20 conjunctions have been replaced by other letters in this cryptolist. Find the letters that were substituted in the original word. Several letters have been given to help you get started. Fill in the remaining letters for each conjunction.

1. JGOVU      = _ _ _ _ _ _

2. YPS        = _ _ _

3. MYOXS      = _ _ _ _ _

4. VY         = _ _

5. GPS        = _ _ _

6. TJO        = _ _ _

7. PS         = _ _

8. OAMG       = _ _ _ _ _

9. KAVUX      = _ _ _ _ _ _

10. EVGRX     = _ _ _ _ _ _

11. TXRMJEX   = _ _ _ _ _ _ _ _

12. JGUXEE    = _ _ _ _ _ _ _

13. KAXG      = _ _ _ _ _

14. MGB       = _ _ _ _

15. OVUU      = _ _ _ _ _

16. PGRX      = _ _ _ _ _

17. MUOAPJHA  = _ _ _ _ _ _ _ _ _

18. ZXO       = _ _ _ _

19. ME        = _ _

20. TXYPSX    = _ _ _ _ _ _ _

*Letter Substitution Code Used:*

| Letter: | A | B | C | D | E | F | G | H | I | J | K | L | M | N | O | P | Q | R | S | T | U | V | W | X | Y | Z |
|---------|---|---|---|---|---|---|---|---|---|---|---|---|---|---|---|---|---|---|---|---|---|---|---|---|---|---|
| Code:   | M | _ | _ | B | _ | _ | _ | A | V | _ | _ | U | _ | _ | P | _ | _ | _ | E | O | _ | _ | _ | _ | _ | _ |

# 2-84. TRANSITIONAL WORDS AND PHRASES

Transitions provide the bridge between ideas. Sometimes these transitional words and phrases connect ideas within a sentence and other times they are used to connect the ideas found in two sentences. Rather than writing two simple sentences such as, "Tony is stocky" and "Tony's brother is slim," the writer can use the transitional word **and** to connect the ideas. The new sentence "Tony is stocky, and his brother is slim" is a more sophisticated sentence. The purpose of the word *and* is **to connect** the two sentences.

Below are 24 transitional expressions. Write each expression on the lines next to its correct purpose. If your answers are correct, each group will have three transitions. If there is time, write an example sentence for each group on the back of this sheet.

| | | | | | |
|---|---|---|---|---|---|
| and | beyond | for instance | in fact | moreover | similarly |
| as a result | consequently | for this reason | in other words | nearby | specifically |
| before | even though | furthermore | in the same manner | nevertheless | that is |
| below | finally | in conclusion | likewise | on the other hand | while |

**to compare:** _____

_____

**to contrast:** _____

_____

**to give examples:** _____

_____

**to indicate logical relationship:** _____

_____

**to show addition:** _____

_____

**to show place or direction:** _____

_____

**to show time:** _____

_____

**to summarize or conclude:** _____

_____

# 2-85. COMBINING SENTENCES

On a separate sheet of paper, combine the sentences in each group into one sentence. When appropriate, use the co-ordinating conjunctions, subordinating conjunctions, and relative pronouns listed below. You may delete and/or add words, but keep the same ideas as found in the original sentences. An example is done for you.

## Coordinating Conjunctions

and     nor
but     or
for

## Relative Pronouns

that    whom
which   whose
who

## Subordinating Conjunctions

| after | because | since | until | where |
|-------|---------|-------|-------|-------|
| although | before | though | when | wherever |
| as | if | unless | whenever | while |

**Example:** The camcorder is expensive. It was purchased at Selmar's Camera Shop. The camcorder has many interesting functions.

**New Sentence:** The expensive camcorder that was purchased at Selmar's Camera Shop has many interesting functions.

**Group One:** The chef is famous. He has worked at this restaurant for twenty years. He prepares many appetizing dinners.

**Group Two:** The phone rang. My sister did not hear it. She was outside talking to her friends.

**Group Three:** The band was outstanding. The audience applauded. The concert was held at Palmer's Stadium. The concert was a sellout.

**Group Four:** The kindergarten class went to the assembly. The assembly lasted for one hour. Three magicians performed during the assembly. The assembly was last Tuesday morning.

**Group Five:** Maureen enjoys surfing the Internet. She was given a computer. Maureen recently graduated from high school. Maureen will use the new computer at college.

# 2-86. MORE SENTENCE COMBINATIONS

Using each of the ten words (or pairs of words) in the box only once, combine each pair of sentences below. These ten words are the only ones you will need to add to combine these sentences. Write the combined sentence on the lines beneath the sentence pair. Use the proper punctuation.

| after | and | either . . . or | in order that | when |
|-------|-----|-----------------|---------------|------|
| although | because | if | unless | who |

1. Keep quiet. Leave.

   _____

2. The car's price is reduced. I am afraid that I cannot afford to buy it.

   _____

3. She knows it is time for her to eat. My cat sees me going to the food cabinet.

   _____

4. She has worked hard and has earned better grades than her classmates. She was rewarded for her efforts.

   _____

5. Mr. Lowney is a truck driver. Mr. Morton is a psychologist.

   _____

6. She is the singer. She has had four hit recordings.

   _____

7. The older man panicked. He heard the blast.

   _____

8. The rain stops. We will perform the play on the outdoor stage.

   _____

9. Both sides act fairly. Mediators will be present at the meeting.

   _____

10. I studied very hard for the test. My score was only 74.

   _____

# 2-87. SUBORDINATION

Main thoughts should be used in independent clauses and subordinate thoughts should be used in dependent clauses. You must decide what is the main thought and what is the subordinate thought so that you place these ideas appropriately. If the two sentences, "The car swerved" and "The car hit the pole" were combined using subordination, the new sentence would read "When the car swerved, it hit the pole." Using the rule of subordination, combine each group of sentences.

1. Henry could not read, and he took reading lessons.

   _____

   _____

2. The papers were delivered two hours late. The snow snarled traffic.

   _____

   _____

3. The class behaved for the substitute teacher. The teacher rewarded the class.

   _____

   _____

4. The superintendent saw the high grass. She ordered the crew to cut the grass immediately.

   _____

   _____

5. Francine was selected for the All-State Orchestra and she plays the oboe very well.

   _____

   _____

6. We wrote to the Complaint Department. We received a letter of apology. The letter was signed by the company president.

   _____

   _____

7. Dick Gregory worked hard. He became a civil rights activist. He also became a famous comedian.

   _____

   _____

8. Jimmy Montego is an outstanding individual. He has been given awards by many groups.

   _____

   _____

9. Shakespeare was an outstanding playwright, and he is famous today. He wrote plays nearly 400 years ago.

   _____

   _____

10. The young lady is beautiful, and she is talented. She was voted Miss America.

    _____

    _____

# 2-88. COORDINATING THE IDEAS

"I like the new house. It is pretty. We moved into it last month." These three sentences seem rather simple when contrasted to the sentence "I like the pretty new house that we moved into last month," which combines all three ideas. Though a simple sentence can be quite effective, a series of simple sentences can be very trying for the reader. Thus, writing mature sentences is the way to go.

Combine the simple sentences in each group into one mature sentence. Use phrases, clauses, conjunctions, and any other coordinating tools you wish. An example is done for you.

**Example:** The car broke down. We borrowed the car from my neighbor. The car is green. It is a station wagon.
**New Sentence:** The green station wagon that we borrowed from my neighbor broke down.

1. We read a story. The story had a surprise ending. A princess was in the story. It was written by Frank Stockton.

   _____

   _____

2. The fireworks show was exciting. My friends and I went to see the show. It was held at the local beach. It lasted for 45 minutes.

   _____

   _____

3. My uncle painted his barn. He painted it last October. He was helped by my cousins. The barn was red. Now it is white.

   _____

   _____

4. Our bus was late. We missed our doctor's appointment. We had to make a new appointment. The new appointment is June 25.

   _____

   _____

5. The drivers were speeding. The road they were on is curvy. The drivers were headed for the exit. The exit is called Van Buren Boulevard.

   _____

   _____

# 2-88. COORDINATING THE IDEAS (cont'd)

6. We will study chemistry this semester. The chemistry teacher is Mrs. Logan. She has been teaching chemistry for ten years. She is an excellent teacher.

_____

_____

7. You need a pass to get into the exposition. The pass costs twelve dollars. The exposition features boats and cars. I can buy the pass for you.

_____

_____

8. Steve Martin is a comedian. He has starred in many movies. He has gray hair. He has a great smile.

_____

_____

9. Kyle went to buy seafood. He took twenty dollars with him. He will buy shrimp and crabs. Our family will eat the seafood that Kyle buys.

_____

_____

10. The lamp broke. A ball hit the lamp. Brett threw the ball. The ball was a volleyball.

_____

_____

On the lines below, write a sentence that combines three ideas. Check your punctuation.

_____

_____

# 2-89. FIFTY PERCENT OF THE TIME

Four original sentences have been combined in ten different ways. Five of the ten combinations are correct. The other five combinations exhibit writing problems including fragments, run-ons, and other mechanical and usage errors. On the space next to the sentence's number, write either **C** if the group of words is a complete sentence or **N** if the words do **not** make a complete sentence. If your answers are correct, the number totals of the complete sentences is 33 while the incomplete sentences total 22.

> The four original sentences that are; (A) The waves crashed on the shore. (B) The swimmers enjoyed themselves. (C) The waves were foamy. (D) Young people and older people were swimming.

1. _____ The swimmers who were both young and older people enjoyed themselves, the waves were foamy and crashed on the shore.

2. _____ Waves, foamy and crashing on the shore, were enjoyed by the swimmers; young and older.

3. _____ Foamy and crashing on the shore, the swimmers, young and older, enjoyed themselves.

4. _____ The young and older swimmers enjoyed themselves as the foamy waves crashed on the shore.

5. _____ The swimmers, who were both young and older, enjoyed themselves in the foamy waves that crashed on the shore.

6. _____ As the foamy waves crashed on the shore, the young and older swimmers enjoyed themselves.

7. _____ Crashed on the shore, the swimmers, young and older, enjoyed the foamy waves.

8. _____ The young and older swimmers enjoyed themselves while the foamy waves crashed on the shore.

9. _____ The foamy waves were enjoyed by the young and older swimmers; the crashing waves also.

10. _____ The young and older swimmers enjoyed themselves in the foamy waves that crashed on the shore.

**Self-check:** Do the five sentences that display a correct combination of the original sentences total 33? Do the five sentences that display an incorrect combination of the original sentences total 22?

© 1999 by The Center for Applied Research in Education

# 2-90. SHOWING YOUR VERSATILITY

By skillfully using a phrase, a clause, or a sentence, the talented writer can express the same thought in different ways. Since variety is important to the writer (and the reader!), it is necessary to know how to manipulate words to attain the desired goal.

If the ideas the writer wanted to relate are that *the Pilgrims landed at Plymouth, Massachusetts in 1620* and that *the Pilgrims wanted religious freedom*, there are several basic ways to express these ideas. Here are some examples:

**Clause within a sentence or a complex sentence:** The Pilgrims who wanted religious freedom landed at Plymouth, Massachusetts, in 1620.
**Verbal phrase within a sentence:** Wanting religious freedom, the Pilgrims landed at Plymouth, Massachusetts in 1620.

Using the suggested methods, combine each group of ideas on a separate piece of paper. Share your answers with your classmates.

**Group #1:** Ms. Sampson is a lawyer. She questioned the witness. The witness was frightened.
  (a) complex sentence      (b) sentence employing a verbal phrase

**Group #2:** Justin went to the town meeting. He became angry. He left after twenty minutes.
  (a) simple sentence using parallelism; (b) sentence using an adjectival clause; (c) sentence using an adverbial clause

**Group #3:** Marie wanted to become an anthropologist. She studied hard.
  (a) sentence using a cause-and-effect idea; (b) sentence using an adjectival clause

**Group #4:** The box office will open at three o'clock. I will buy our concert tickets at the box office. I will use my credit card to buy our concert tickets.
  (a) complex sentence beginning with an adverbial clause; (b) sentence using a verbal phrase

**Group #5:** I finished the puzzle. The puzzle was easy. The puzzle took me fifteen minutes to solve.
  (a) simple sentence; (b) complex sentence

# ANSWER KEY

## 2-1. WHAT WILL A MOUSE DO?

| | | |
|---|---|---|
| 1. A | 5. A | 9. C |
| 2. T | 6. C | 10. A |
| 3. T | 7. T | 11. T |
| 4. R | 8. A | |

What will a mouse do? ATTRACT A CAT

## 2-2. THREE OF A KIND

1. The man in the blue suit is my father's best friend.
   (1 = The, 2 = blue, 2 = best)

2. The doctor slowly handed me the instrument near the machine.
   (3 = doctor, 6 = slowly, 5 = handed, 9 me, 8 = instrument, 7 = near the machine)

3. Those who forget the past will be in trouble in the future.
   (10 = who forget the past, 4 = will, 5 = be)

4. Each of the people in the room knows your sister's fame.
   (3 = Each, 8 = fame)

5. The talented architect who designed this city gained lasting fame because of his feat.
   (10 = who designed this city, 5 = gained, 2 = lasting)

6. Lately I have not been feeling well and think I should see a doctor.
   (6 = Lately, 4 = have, 5 = feeling)

7. The painting that is hanging in the adjacent room was a gift to the embassy.
   (10 = that is hanging in the adjacent room, 7 = to the embassy)

8. He gave me a chance to take the last shot in the game.
   (3 = He, 9 = me, 1 = a)

9. An intelligent decision must be made immediately in this case.
   (1 = An, 6 = immediately)

10. Justin will be studying physical therapy for the next three years.
    (4 = be, 8 = physical therapy, 7 = for the next three years)

## 2-3. LOOKING INTO THE HEART OF THE SENTENCE

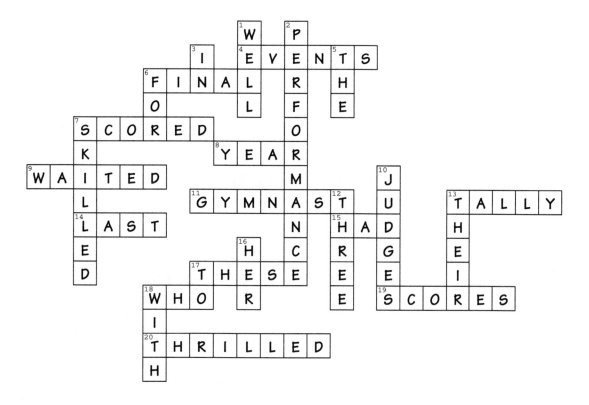

## 2-4. THE TERMS OF THE SENTENCE

## 2-5. FITTING THE PIECES TOGETHER

| | |
|---|---|
| 1. ME | 5. US |
| 2. TI | 6. SL |
| 3. CU | 7. OP |
| 4. LO | 8. PY |

Word: METICULOUS; antonym: SLOPPY.

## 2-6. PUTTING IT ALL TOGETHER

Answers will vary.

## 2-7. WE HAVE ATTITUDES! FIFTEEN OF THEM!!!

Answers will vary.

## 2-8. MOOD SENTENCES

Answers will vary.

## 2-9. THE PERIODIC SENTENCE

Answers will vary.

## 2-10. A STARTER SENTENCE'S PURPOSE

Answers will vary.

## 2-11. STRENGTHENING YOUR SENTENCES

Answers will vary. These are suggestions.

1. Jerry spoke confidently and intelligently with his understanding father in the quiet den.
2. Seeing the hunters, the astute cheetah ran into the woods.
3. A blue car swiftly passed us in the afternoon.
4. After the game was over, the injured soccer player walked and joked with her teammate outside the gymnasium.

5. My older sister and my mother traveled to Europe during the winter.

6. The new movie that was filmed in Canada is exciting and intelligent.

7. She completed yesterday's crossword puzzle in only fifteen minutes.

8. Because the wind was strong, the umbrella blew over.

9. He and I saw the black Jeep.

10. Desmond was the last man to win that award.

## 2-12. COP AN ATTITUDE

The topic is listed first; the attitude follows.

1. mother; interesting

2. rock group's performance; outrageous

3. words; inspirational

4. spending all that money on a new car; foolish

5. movie; boring

6. presentation of the new material; soporific

7. office manager; efficient

8. Trying to convince his mother to allow him to go skiing with his friends that weekend; exercise in futility

9. response to our question; shocking

10. The New York Times articles; intellectually stimulating

11. Mr. Bergen's health class; challenging

12. mosquitoes' infestation; annoyance

13. Laurie's way of looking at the situation; strange

14. Driving to work each morning; taxing

15. method of taking care of matters; uncanny

## 2-13. MAKING OBSERVATIONS

Answers will vary.

## 2-14. DESCRIPTIONS OF PEOPLE

Answers will vary.

## 2-15. MORE DESCRIPTIONS OF PEOPLE

Answers will vary.


## 2-16. POETIC DESCRIPTIONS

Answers will vary.


## 2-17. MAKING SENSE (AND SENTENCES) OUT OF POETRY

Answers will vary.


## 2-18. STRUCTURING YOUR SENTENCES

Answers will vary. These are suggestions.

1. The family that moved into our neighborhood has four young children.
2. Since the church's steeple is quite high, the roofer had a difficult time nailing the shingles on it.
3. Walking to the park takes a long time, but it is good exercise.
4. Thirty minutes after the Hudsons broke down on the highway, the tow truck arrived, and they paid the tow truck driver 70 dollars to tow them back to his garage.
5. Those trees giving good shade are weeping willows.
6. The doctor told us the good news, and then we celebrated.
7. Because our desk drawer is messy, we could not find the license application, and we had to go to the county office for another application.
8. The almost unbearable weather made us have two air conditioners and three fans working in our house.
9. Since the stapler was jammed, he could not staple his term paper's 12 pages.
10. His stapler was jammed, and he could not staple his term paper's 12 pages.


## 2-19. HOW SIMPLE? HOW COMPOUND? HOW COMPLEX?

1. CPLX
2. CPD
3. CC
4. S
5. CPLX
6. CC
7. S

   8. CPD
   9. CC
   10. S
   11. CPLX
   12. CPD

## 2-20.  STAYING SIMPLE FOR STARTERS

The subject is listed first, then main verb.

1. warden, handed
2. All, talked
3. song, took
4. hawk, elevated
5. War, overtook
6. realization, lingered
7. days, speed
8. linguist, articulated
9. region, generated
10. estimates, seem
11. three, called
12. ovation, numbed
13. Thinking, intrigues
14. None, eat
15. nonconformist, traveled
16. ascent, scared
17. investigation, astound

What's the world's largest continent? ASIA.

## 2-21.  MAIN VERBS

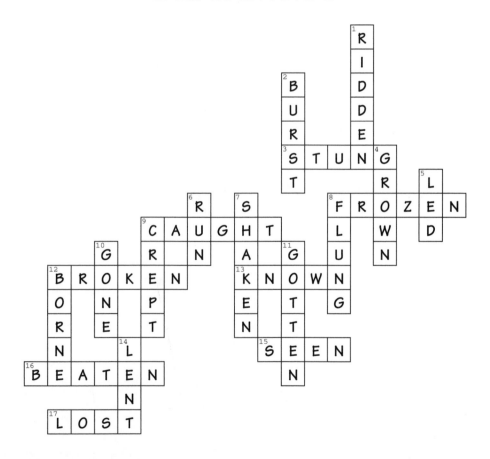

## 2-22. LIFE'S BIG QUESTION

The verb is listed after the subject.

1. workers; offered
2. umbrellas; lined
3. driver; yelling
4. officers; understood
5. raccoon; attacked
6. temperature; hit
7. earl; recounted
8. boom; echoed
9. harbor; emptied
10. airplanes; landed
11. tragedy; happened
12. you; offered
13. recorder; worked
14. each; accepted
15. Leroy; told
16. hitter; yelled

**Life's big question:** Would you rather be healthy or wealthy?

## 2-23. PARTS-OF-SPEECH TRIOS

| | | | |
|---|---|---|---|
| 1. p | 7. prep | 13. n | 19. adj |
| 2. prep | 8. p | 14. i | 20. n |
| 3. v | 9. c | 15. adv | 21. v |
| 4. adj | 10. v | 16. i | 22. adj |
| 5. n | 11. adv | 17. i | 23. prep |
| 6. adv | 12. c | 18. c | 24. p |

## 2-24. FIVE EACH

```
R D V P G W C S W Y C V Q K M R T L P X S J B Z
F C X Q T B V K O Y B L C D S L S Y S B J Z N B
P H V N H D W C D L N A D M K J V T H Z P T X N
R V K K E D K S K E I M U N G W R V R B F B K M
Z R F B M R L R K Y V D R T J R C S E O V R Z M
X N T L S F J T M Q S I L E O Q O Z Q R N A A Y
M I N T E L L I G E N T L Y W M M W Y K Y G R B
I K S M L S J F J A Z Q E I C A O N T F A M E Z
N T Q P V C R V S V N H D F S N R B I Z H S Q S
E I N F E S T U O Z T G S L D H D D I R O Y U H
H H R P S A O S N L C R E T L I N E L L U I C
C D G Q M U K Q C Y D R R Y C L E T V N E K R X
F G D L N K K E X D L F N Q O B U D O F F W E S
X Y R E D X N P R T U R C S J P L G Q Z V H H H
Q G R N S X V D Q L C V Z B M X V R R B R B X N
D T V X J D R Z L R R J N O D K P Z R N Z M R H
S V Z N T Q G Z V C R J C B P D K K B P L Z N J
```

angry  __adjective__

automobile  __noun__

brag __verb__

computer __noun__

devilish __adjective__

drawer __noun__

grow __verb__

infest __verb__

intelligently __adverb__

magazine __noun__

mine __pronoun__

only __adverb__

ours __pronoun__

require __verb__

so __adverb__

solidify __verb__

solidly __adverb__

speaker __noun__

strenuous __adjective__

strong __adjective__

themselves __pronoun__

they __pronoun__

very __adverb__

wonderful __adjective__

yourself __pronoun__

## 2-25. DOUBLE-DUTY WORDS

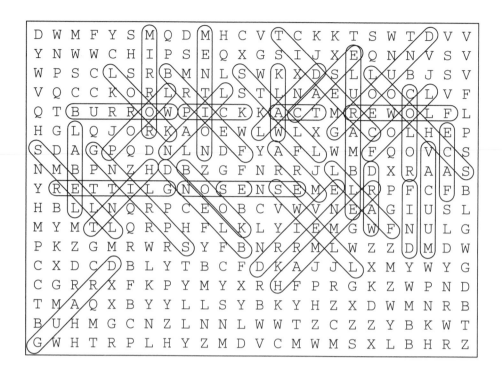

## 2-26. SENTENCE ASSOCIATES

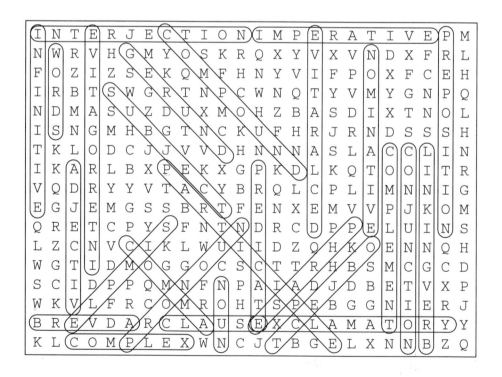

## 2-27. ADJECTIVES, ADVERBS, AND SPELLING

1. clear
2. frozen
3. now
4. pretty
5. soon
6. fiercely
7. well
8. rigid
9. rarely
10. only
11. carefully
12. swiftly
13. whenever
14. robust
15. slowly
16. powerfully
17. astute
18. better
19. muscular
20. tall

*Letter identification code:*

A B C D E F G H I J K L M N O P Q R S T U V W X Y Z
G E B W X H P I F D J Y T M V C S N L K Z A U O R Q

## 2-28. PARTS-OF-SPEECH FILL-INS

Answers will vary. These are suggestions.

1. Louisa moved into the apartment.
2. He slowly walked with her.
3. Will she help with your assignment?
4. Are you going now?
5. He and they can work my booth.
6. Carry the dishes carefully.
7. Because John is tall, he can win.
8. You and I will succeed if we try.

## 2-29. WORKING YOUR WAY THROUGH THE PARTS OF SPEECH

Answers will vary. These are suggestions.

1. Our valedictorian became a cardiologist.
2. It was exceptional and beautiful.
3. They were ready for some soulful music.
4. This has been a great day.
5. They could play immediately.
6. Although he tried, they ignored his efforts.
7. He walked into the crowded room.
8. The animal has distinct advantages over the other animals.
9. Neither the girl nor the officers saw her sister.
10. Slowly and confidently, Kenny moved the valuable antique.

## 2-30. MORE PARTS-OF-SPEECH FILL-INS

Answers will vary.

## 2-31. MATCH THE SENTENCE WITH ITS DESCRIPTION

1. J        6. H
2. F        7. D
3. A        8. E
4. G        9. I
5. C        10. B

## 2-32. DISSECTING THE SENTENCE

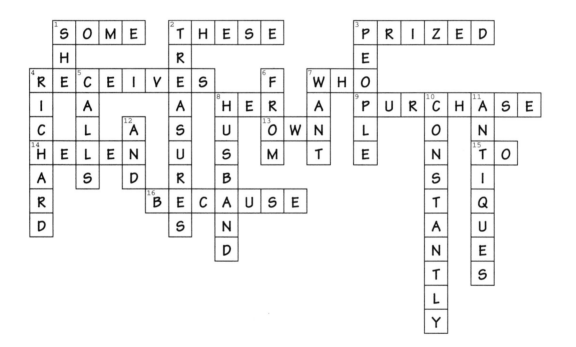

## 2-33. FINDING THE 21 VERB PHRASES

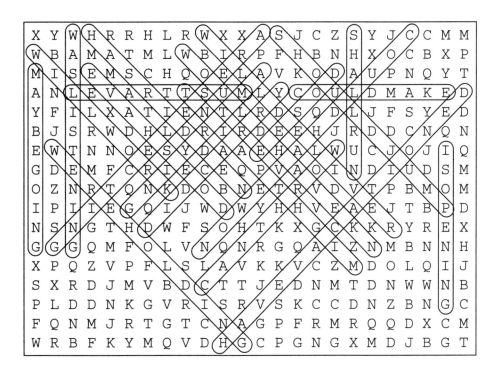

## 2-34. PLACING THE PREPOSITIONAL PHRASES

| | | |
|---|---|---|
| 1. J | 6. I | 11. H |
| 2. D | 7. L | 12. G |
| 3. N | 8. M | 13. O |
| 4. F | 9. B | 14. K |
| 5. A | 10. E | 15. C |

## 2-35. LOCATING VERBAL PHRASES

*Five gerund phrases (in order):* Saving another person's life; Seeing the helpless eight-year-old swimmer; Reaching this boy in time; rescuing young bathers; Handing her first rescue to his family.

*Five infinitive phrases (in order):* to make her a heroine for her bravery; to remember; to regain his composure; to run swiftly; to signal to him.

*Five participial phrases (in order):* Walking back toward her stand near the shoreline; recalling the details; disregarding his mother's warnings; Taken by the current; grabbing her line and a life preserver

## 2-36. VERBALS VYING FOR VICTORY

1. (I) To become a better speaker
2. (P) Living in an apartment with her friends

3. (N)

4. (P) Leaving early

5. (N)

6. (I) to think more intensely

7. (G) working diligently

8. (G) Handing out the flyers at the convention

9. (N)

10. (P) Handing out the flyers at the convention

11. (G) her thinking

12. (P) racing down the road

13. (P) Remembering her friend's birthday

14. (P) broadcast in over seventy countries

15. (P) sprinting after his grandchildren

Participles: 7 times

Gerunds: 3 times.

Infinitives: 2 times.

# 2-37. FINDING THE 15 PHRASES

1. (P) Refreshing her memory

2. (A) one of the New England States

3. (ADV) from a distance

4. (ADV) in her hotel room

5. (G) Realizing the fatal flaw

6. (ADJ) in the striped shirt

7. (I) to win the final category

8. (ADJ) in Montana

9. (A) the eloquent speaker

10. (I) to make a deli run

11. (G) Hiking this challenging mountain

12. (ADV) after the service

13. (ADJ) from your sister

14. (A) the newest choir member

15. (P) pushing the train door

## 2-38. AN OLYMPIAN EXPERIENCE

| | | | |
|---|---|---|---|
| 1. | B | 10. | M |
| 2. | A | 11. | U |
| 3. | R | 12. | N |
| 4. | C | 13. | I |
| 5. | E | 14. | C |
| 6. | L | 15. | H |
| 7. | O | | |
| 8. | N | | |
| 9. | A | | |

Letters spell out BARCELONA and MUNICH, two cities that hosted the Olympics.

## 2-39. SHOWING VARIETY WITHIN YOUR SENTENCES

Answers will vary.

## 2-40. THE CLAUSE COURSE

| | | | | | |
|---|---|---|---|---|---|
| 1. | 1 | 6. | 1 | 11. | 2 |
| 2. | 2 | 7. | 3 | 12. | 1 |
| 3. | 3 | 8. | 3 | 13. | 3 |
| 4. | 3 | 9. | 1 | 14. | 1 |
| 5. | 2 | 10. | 2 | 15. | 2 |

*First place:* 15 points; noun clause
*Second place:* 10 points; adverbial clause
*Third place:* 5 points; adjectival clause

# 2-41. FINDING THE DEPENDENT
## OR SUBORDINATE CLAUSES

Students' sentences will vary.

# 2-42. MAKING TWO INTO ONE

1. TOL
2. OVE
3. IST
4. ORE
5. CEI
6. VEA
7. GLI
8. MPS
9. EOF
10. HEA
11. VEN

TO LOVE IS TO RECEIVE A GLIMPSE OF HEAVEN.—Karen Sunde

# 2-43. WISE WORDS FROM WISE WOMEN

1. F
2. B
3. C
4. I
5. J
6. L
7. A
8. G
9. D
10. H
11. K
12. E

## 2-44. DOUBLE THE SCORE

| | | |
|---|---|---|
| 1. P | 6. SC | 11. P |
| 2. P | 7. SEN | 12. P |
| 3. P | 8. SEN | 13. P |
| 4. P | 9. SC | 14. P |
| 5. P | 10. SEN | 15. P |

*Sentences and Subordinate Clauses:* Total:—40

*Phrases:* Total:—80

## 2-45. DEVELOPING A STORY THROUGH PHRASES

Stories will vary. Check that the phrases are used correctly.

## 2-46. FILLING IN THE FRAGMENTS

Answers will vary.

## 2-47. ADD TO, TAKE FROM, OR MAKE ANOTHER CHANGE

Answers will vary.

## 2-48. JIVE WITH FIVE

| | | |
|---|---|---|
| 1. S | 6. S | 11. S |
| 2. F | 7. F | 12. RO |
| 3. F | 8. S | 13. F |
| 4. RO | 9. RO | 14. S |
| 5. F | 10. RO | 15. RO |

## 2-49. KNOWING WHEN A GROUP OF WORDS IS A SENTENCE

| | | |
|---|---|---|
| 1. S (1 point) | 6. RO (6 points) | 11. RO (11 points) |
| 2. RO (2 points) | 7. F (7 points) | 12. S (12 points) |
| 3. F (3 points) | 8. S (8 points) | 13. S (13 points) |
| 4. RO (4 points) | 9. RO (9 points) | 14. F (14 points) |
| 5. F (5 points) | 10. S (10 points) | 15. F (15 points) |

S = 1 + 8 + 10 + 12 + 13 = 44

F = 3 + 5 + 7 + 14 + 15 = 44

RO = 2 + 4 + 6 + 9 +11 = 32

## 2-50. RUNNING DOWN THE RUN-ON SENTENCE

Answers will vary. These are suggestions.

1. . . . house, and we . . .
2. . . . players; he . . .
3. . . . shoulder; for . . .
4. . . . hurry since we . . .
5. . . . information. If . . .
6. . . . me. Responsibility . . .
7. . . . yourself because you . . .
8. . . . aunt who . . .
9. . . . country; it . . .
10. . . . race, and then . . .
11. . . . fun. It made . . .
12. . . . deceptive because it . . .
13. . . . light since it . . .
14. . . . program because we . . .
15. . . . wall. They . . .

## 2-51. WHERE DID THE OTHER WORDS GO?

Answers will vary.

## 2-52. TOO MANY WORDS

Answers will vary. These are suggestions.

1. This orchestra's musicians play beautifully.
2. Each violinist studied many years.
3. These men and women musicians are both experienced and skilled.
4. Seventy people are in this orchestra.
5. We heard their music.
6. My friend is now studying to become a musician.
7. The high school orchestra's members are older than we.
8. If Shane becomes a famous musician, we will celebrate that joyous occasion.
9. The school's music teacher, Mrs. Harvey, has often praised Shane.
10. Because Shane is a talented, diligent, and persevering musician, he might become a member of the Boston Pops.

## 2-53. KEEP IT SIMPLE

Answers will vary. These are suggestions.

1. The intelligent woman phoned her daughter.
2. Harry laughed and held his stomach.
3. Use common sense in dangerous situations.

4. Turk bikes and hikes in the afternoon.
5. Please send me your college's admissions application.
6. Some of my school's orchestra's members want to go on the class trip to Canada.
7. Mary purchased the blouse she is wearing last August.
8. Uncle Jerry gave Dad a car.
9. The Youth Corps repainted the building built in 1939.
10. You are wearing your older brother's former shoes.

# 2-54. WORDINESS IS OUT

Answers will vary. These are suggestions.

1. We have no immediate plans.
2. He would not fit in here.
3. Because Judy is talented, she can do it.
4. Because Hector is strong, he can lift that heavy rock.
5. Regina will be the new clarinet player.
6. Always keep your hands inside the car.
7. A statement just came from the president's office.
8. Hank Smith's comedy was the hit of the recent film festival.
9. She loves to attract attention.
10. Teenagers must complete this form to vote in next year's election.
11. Transplanting an organ amazes me.
12. The game will be won with a field goal.

# 2-55. LET'S NOT OVERSTATE IT

Answers will vary. These are suggestions.

1. (*concern*) We were worried about my cousin when we learned he had been in a traffic accident.
2. (*happiness*) She sprinted home to tell her mother the exciting news.
3. (*ecstasy*) After winning the lottery and quitting his boring job, Kyle felt life could not be any better.
4. (*frustration*) Following many unsuccessful attempts to fix the machine, the mechanic smashed the wrench on the bench.
5. (*fatigue*) The marathon runner's legs felt like two cement blocks.
6. (*uncertainty*) Our teacher's puzzled expression following Brian's comment spoke volumes.
7. (*poise*) Smiling confidently and looking directly at the audience, the salutatorian began her graduation speech.

8. (*anger*) Throwing the bat against the backstop, the batter accosted the umpire who just called him out.

9. (*fright*) With both his legs and his heart pumping ferociously, the boy sprinted away from the members of the rival gang.

10. (*loneliness*) Sitting by herself on the shores of the darkened beach, the young girl felt as though there was no one who understood her.

11. (*embarrassment*) After spilling the ravioli on his shirt in the school cafeteria, Marty, hearing the loud laughter of the other students, wished he could crawl into a hole.

12. (*conceit*) The rock star told the reporters that he made more in one concert than they would make in their entire career.

## 2-56. ONE'S RIGHT AND ONE'S WRONG

The letters corresponding to the correctly written sentences spell out WINCHESTER. Winchester Cathedral is the famous place and Winchester is a type of rifle. The corrections necessary in the incorrectly written sentences are as follows.

1. (T) There is more than one way to do this.
2. (O) Both brothers are taller than I.
3. (D) My brother and I will be going with you.
4. (E) The group of words is a fragment.
5. (I) He went to the store and bought a pair of pants.
6. (S) It's the principle of the thing that bothers me.
7. (O) He enjoys bowling, biking, and visiting his grandmother.
8. (W) They divided the candy among the four children.
9. (N) They're correct in saying that.
10. (E) The group of words is a fragment

## 2-57. THE 49'ERS

The following words have commas inserted after them.

**Group One** (24 is the group's total)

1. area
2. president . . . Challie . . . Nashua

**Group Two** (23 is the group's total)

1. tonight
2. bowl . . . ski

**Group Three** (25 is the group's total)

1. truth
2. train
3. math . . . science

**Group Four** (26 is the group's total)

1. late
2. room
3. Moepuffs . . . artist
4. Atlanta

## 2-58. DETECTING SENTENCE ERRORS

| | | | |
|---|---|---|---|
| 1. 5 | 6. 1 | 11. 5 | 16. 1 |
| 2. 4 | 7. 2 | 12. 4 | 17. 2 |
| 3. 3 | 8. 3 | 13. 3 | 18. 3 |
| 4. 2 | 9. 4 | 14. 2 | 19. 4 |
| 5. 1 | 10. 5 | 15. 1 | 20. 5 |

Here are the corrections.

2. I had eaten enough to satisfy two people.
3. He and I are going swimming in the lake.
4. The oysters in the ocean are beautiful.
5. Washing the dishes, I heard the phone ring.
6. We saw the flowers while we were walking to school yesterday.
7. Peanut butter and jelly is my favorite kind of sandwich.
8. I am taller than he.
9. We could have won the game.
12. We had swum in the Atlantic two years ago.
13. The gift was given to Gina and me.
14. Neither the girls nor their brother was going to the airport.
15. To become a good baseball pitcher, one must throw the ball with speed and accuracy.
16. Hurrying to the meeting, the woman dropped her portfolio in the hallway.
17. One of the mechanics is going on vacation next week.
18. The group members did the entire project by themselves.
19. We found that the dryer had shrunk the shirt.

## 2-59. CUTTING OUT THE CONFUSION

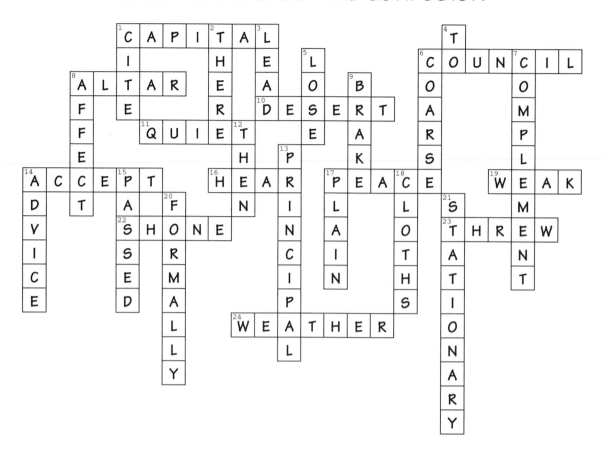

## 2-60. AVOIDING THE PASSIVE VOICE

Answers will vary.

## 2-61. ANIMALS IN SIMILES

| | | |
|---|---|---|
| 1. H | 6. A | 11. O |
| 2. B | 7. N | 12. K |
| 3. D | 8. I | 13. J |
| 4. M | 9. F | 14. E |
| 5. G | 10. L | 15. C |

## 2-62. KICKING OUT THE CLICHÉS

Answers will vary. These are suggestions.

1. I will always be your friend.
2. After training hard for so many years, Bob was physically fit.
3. Molly's new infant is light.

4. She often found herself in a bad situation.

5. The doctor told the heavy drinker that he should stop drinking.

6. They told us an old story.

7. Needless to say, her performance proved that she was not feeling well.

8. Now that your parents have seen your grades, you should be on your best behavior.

9. Those merchants charge high prices.

10. Your artistic talent is recognizable.

11. Upon receiving the news, Martin was very happy.

12. Watch out! That man is shrewd.

13. Professor Prescott knows the procedure very well.

14. Those two are much alike.

15. Last weekend it rained heavily on the mainland.

# 2-63. EXPLAINING THE IDIOMS

Answers will vary. These are suggestions.

2. Juanita felt that she was in a difficult position.

3. It was a miracle.

4. She felt that she had to accept something burdensome.

5. Unfortunately for the team members, it was time to confront the situation.

6. Both families decided to make peace.

7. Kevin completely believed our story.

8. After only a few minutes of the contest, I knew I was overmatched.

9. This was my chance to do two things at once.

10. It was a case of name-calling.

11. Don't you think that you are injuring your own interests?

12. Roberta felt that her job placed her in an enviable position.

13. Steven had said the wrong thing too many times.

14. The detectives were cautious.

15. Pay close attention to what others around you are thinking and saying.

# 2-64. THREE-WORD SENTENCES

Answers will vary. These are suggestions.

| | |
|---|---|
| Active acrobats appear. | Diligent druggists deliver. |
| Bulky bodybuilders boast. | Eloquent eulogies enchant. |
| Conscientious cardiologists care. | Fluent Frenchmen forget. |

Glamorous girls glide.

Handsome husbands hurry.

Intelligent industrialists insist.

Jovial journalists jest.

Kind kittens kiss.

Lovely leprechauns left.

Minute microorganisms multiplied.

Noisy nomads noticed.

Old operators opined.

Peculiar powers persisted.

Querulous quarterbacks quarreled.

Raucous raconteurs revel.

Strong stevedores survive.

Terrified turncoats trembled.

Uninformed urchins united.

Vicious vendors voted.

Wicked witches wrangled.

Xanthous xenophiles x-rayed.

Youthful yeomen yelled.

Zany zoologists zagged.

## 2-65. SCRAMBLED SENTENCES

1. Did the glass shatter?
2. Before you go, please lock the door.
3. Our coach told us to warm up for fifteen minutes.
4. Since the water is warm, let's go swimming.
5. Both cars are in the repair shop.
6. Will this fan cool the entire room?
7. The hammock is in the garage.
8. Seal the envelope and then mail it.
9. The movie is a drama about police officers and their work.
10. These new CD's are the best I have ever bought.
11. The firm wants to hire both of you.
12. We will meet you after your soccer game.

## 2-66. JOINING WORDS TO MAKE SENTENCES

Answers will vary. These are suggestions.

1. She swiftly ran around the track.
2. Why don't you call her again?
3. This is probably the last time I will see you this summer.
4. What is your favorite musical group?
5. Three drivers were stopped for speeding on Hillside Avenue.
6. Tell me what you would like to do tomorrow night.
7. Unless you take your time, you might make a critical mistake.
8. If he took any pride in what he does, he could be a terrific player.
9. You might as well let us know what we must do.
10. Is there any suggestion of wrongdoing here?

## 2-67. CONSTRUCTING THE SENTENCES

Allow for discussion.

| | | |
|---|---|---|
| A—K—I | E—I—F | I—D—K |
| B—L—C | F—B—E | J—G—J |
| C—J—H | G—C—G | K—H—D |
| D—E—A | H—A—B | L—F—L |

## 2-68. CONSECUTIVE LETTERS

Answers will vary. These are suggestions.

1. An old plumber quit.
2. An intelligent jokester kidded.
3. A brave cat dashed.
4. An unusual violin warped.
5. The frightened girls hurried.
6. The lonely man noticed.
7. An awkward baboon climbed.
8. The jovial kid laughed.
9. A caring doctor explained.
10. The troubled umpire vented.
11. A special teacher understood.
12. An entertaining friend guffawed.
13. A gracious hostess intervened.
14. A dreadful evening followed.
15. A kind librarian motioned.
16. The pretty queen rejoiced.
17. The healthy instructor jogged.
18. A zany acrobat bellowed.
19. The young zebra arose.
20. An elegant female gleamed.

## 2-69. THE PROPER ARRANGEMENT

1. Dinner was served promptly at seven o'clock.
2. They had received funds from different groups.
3. At least seventy people were stranded by the storm.
4. The humorous student could easily make his teachers laugh.

5. Dealing with a declining economy is challenging.
6. Our officials invited foreign dignitaries to our town's bicentennial.
7. We can't build houses fast enough to accommodate the rising population.
8. Bobby and most of his colleagues asked for pay raises.
9. Be sure to cook these clams before eating them.
10. Hidden charges produced confusing new fees for the customers.

## 2-70. CPR FOR THESE SENTENCES!

Answers will vary.

## 2-71. USING MODIFIERS EFFECTIVELY

Answers will vary.

## 2-72. MATCHING THE DEPENDENTS WITH THE INDEPENDENTS

| | | | |
|---|---|---|---|
| 1. F | | 6. G |
| 2. A | | 7. H |
| 3. B | | 8. I |
| 4. J | | 9. C |
| 5. E | | 10. D |

## 2-73. MATCHING THE CAUSE AND THE EFFECT

These are possible, logical answers; there may be others. Invite discussion.

1. Because Harrison Ford is such a terrific actor, his movies are big money-makers.
2. Because he reads slowly, he takes a long time to finish a novel. (Or) He takes a long time to finish a novel because he reads slowly.
3. Because her mom died last year, Janice has had to take on more responsibility.
4. Because it was raining, we could not go sailing. (Or) We could not go sailing because it was raining.
5. Because she has a great sense of humor, she was voted Class Clown. (Or) She was voted Class Clown because she has a great sense of humor.
6. Because Terry is an outstanding athlete, she was given a sports scholarship to college.
7. In order to hear the sound, we turned up the volume. (Or) We turned up the volume in order to hear the sound.

8. He could not use his credit card since it was stolen.

9. So that they could make more money, the band members played longer. **(Or)** The band members played longer so that they could make more money.

10. You cannot get into the concert unless you have a ticket. **(Or)** Unless you have a ticket, you cannot get into the concert.

# 2-74. ADDING TO THE SENTENCE BASE

Answers will vary. These are suggestions.

        adj.                     dep. cl.                     prep. phrase
1. The <u>large</u> group <u>that had been formed twenty years ago</u> was divided <u>on the land purchase issue.</u>

                  dep. clause           m.v.    advb.
2. The bicycle <u>that we had recently purchased</u> was <u>resting</u> <u>perfectly</u> on the car's roof.

               subject               advb.
3. Francine and <u>her sister</u> like to work out <u>vigorously</u> in the morning.

       adj.          advb.   prep. phrase    dep. clause
4. The <u>older</u> cat meowed <u>softly</u> <u>near the hearth</u> <u>that dad had just built.</u>

      adj.             advb  prep. ph.      adverbial clause
5. My <u>younger</u> brother cried <u>softly</u> <u>in his room</u> <u>when he heard the news of Grandpa's death.</u>

# 2-75. FOLLOW-UP SENTENCES

Answers will vary.

# 2-76. DETAILS NEVER HURT

Answers will vary.

# 2-77. CONNECTING THE WORDS

Tomorrow morning our group will visit the Museum of Natural History. Then we will go to see a Broadway show. Finally we will travel home.

# 2-78. PUTTING THEM BACK TOGETHER

Doctor Samson diagnosed the case as mononucleosis.

A blue car sped down the road.

Her family is leaving for vacation tomorrow.

## 2-79. FOLLOWING A HARDER PATH

He plans his work schedule so that his family and he can travel to various exotic places. They have traveled to seven countries this year.

## 2-80. FOUR SENTENCES

The sixteen boys were playing in the park.

All of the doctors were called into the emergency room.

The herd of cows had grazed in the fields.

An elderly woman crossed our street.

Sample bonus answer: Roberto and Juan joked and laughed with each other in the train.

## 2-81. TRANSITIONAL WORDS WORD-FIND

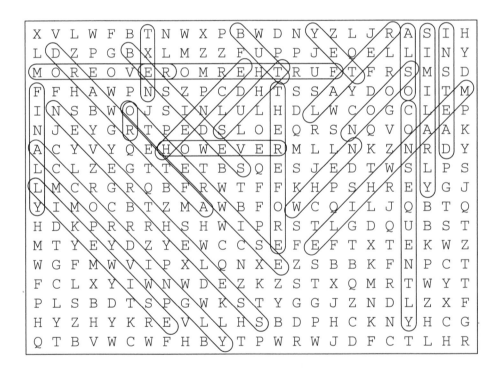

## 2-82. SUBORDINATING CONJUNCTIONS WORD-FIND PUZZLE

```
L F D J C R W A H T K J G T S N S P N X Y H Y H
C I Z E R H E D F D J B T N C P N C A F H X P C
Y G T C E W V V J T F F M G A D V B H D H Z N H
W H E N E V E R F K E Z X N S D N Z T Z B F G Y
H H H O U G N N L L C R O F J X P A R L I U Y C
E I I P W V T W V L N X K H N X H K E N O X S J
R N F L H B H J W W I O T Y X T C N H H K G H N
E O L B E F O R E X S T T R X E T N T S B W N G
A R T N R R U S V M K X X D S X O L A R L A L N
S D Q G E C G L M G D T Z U S T A R R K H B G F
K E N K N M H N C H T Z A R G S N S G T R M B P
J R R L M M P K W H X C N M P V S F V Z N K X P
F T J J Y J W L L K E F H P V L V W W S R Z Z K
B H C Z J L L Y C B N Q N H T S F B K V N H M Z
B A Y P S Q R Y Y H Z M Y W H Q Y Q N W M Z V B
P T H M P V Q F P D H L P C Z C J G Q Z B S X K
Z L G L T K K F T G K J P C C X R Q L J H T P L
```

## 2-83. CRYPTIC CONJUNCTIONS

1. UNTIL
2. FOR
3. AFTER
4. IF
5. NOR
6. BUT
7. OR
8. THAN
9. WHILE
10. SINCE
11. BECAUSE
12. UNLESS
13. WHEN
14. AND
15. TILL
16. ONCE
17. ALTHOUGH
18. YET
19. AS
20. BEFORE

*Letter:* A B C D E F G H I J K L M N O P Q R S T U V W X Y Z
*Code:* M T R B X Y H A V F L U D G P C N S E O J W K I Z Q

## 2-84. TRANSITIONAL WORDS AND PHRASES

**to compare:** in the same manner; likewise; similarly

**to contrast:** even though; nevertheless; on the other hand

**to give examples:** for instance; in fact; specifically

**to indicate logical relationship:** as a result; consequently; for this reason

**to show addition:** and, furthermore; moreover

**to show place or direction:** below; beyond; nearby

**to show time:** before; finally; while

**to summarize or conclude:** in conclusion; in other words; that is

## 2-85. COMBINING SENTENCES

Answers will vary. These are suggestions.

**Group One:** The famous chef, who has worked at this restaurant for twenty years, prepares many appetizing dinners.

**Group Two:** Because my sister was outside talking to her friends, she did not hear the phone ring.

**Group Three:** The audience applauded the outstanding band at the Palmer's Stadium concert.

**Group Four:** Last Tuesday, the kindergarten class went to the one-hour assembly where three magicians performed.

**Group Five:** Maureen, who has recently graduated from high school and enjoys surfing the Internet, was given a computer that she will use at college.

## 2-86. MORE SENTENCE COMBINATIONS

Answers will vary. These are suggestions.

1. *Either* keep quiet *or* leave.
2. *Unless* the car's price is reduced, I am afraid that I cannot afford to buy it.
3. *When* my cat sees me going to the food cabinet, she knows it is time for her to eat.
4. The fourth grader has been rewarded for her efforts *because* she has worked hard and has earned better grades than her classmates.
5. Mr. Lowney is a truck driver, *and* Mr. Morton is a psychologist.
6. She is the singer *who* has had four hit recordings.
7. *After* he heard the loud blast, the older man panicked.
8. *If* the rain stops, we will perform the play on the outdoor stage.
9. *In order that* both sides act fairly, mediators will be present at the meeting.
10. *Although* I studied very hard for the test, my score was only 74.

## 2-87. SUBORDINATION

Answers will vary. These are suggestions.

1. Since Henry could not read, he took reading lessons.
2. The papers were delivered two hours late because the snow had snarled traffic.
3. The teacher rewarded the class for they had behaved for the substitute teacher.
4. After she saw the high grass, the superintendent ordered the crew to cut the grass immediately.
5. Since she plays the oboe very well, Francine was selected for the All-State Orchestra.
6. After we wrote to the Complaint Department, we received a letter of apology signed by the company president.
7. Because he worked hard, Dick Gregory became a civil rights activist and a famous comedian.
8. Jimmy Montego, who is an outstanding individual, has been given awards by many groups.
9. Even though he wrote plays nearly 400 years ago, Shakespeare, an outstanding playwright, is famous today.
10. Because the young lady is beautiful and talented, she was voted Miss America.

## 2-88. COORDINATING THE IDEAS

Answers will vary. These are suggestions.

1. We read Frank Stockton's story that included a princess and a surprise ending.
2. My friends and I went to the local beach to see the exciting fireworks show that lasted 45 minutes.
3. Last October my uncle and cousins painted his red barn white.
4. Because our bus was late, we missed our doctor's appointment and rescheduled another appointment for June 25.
5. Speeding on the curvy road, the drivers were headed for the Van Buren Boulevard exit.
6. Next semester we will study chemistry with Mrs. Logan, an excellent teacher who has been teaching chemistry for ten years.
7. I can buy the twelve-dollar pass you need to get into the boats and cars exposition.
8. Steve Martin, the gray-haired comedian who has starred in many movies, has a great smile.
9. Taking twenty dollars along, Kyle went to buy the shrimp and crabs that our family will eat.
10. Brett threw the volleyball that hit and broke the lamp.

# 2-89. FIFTY PERCENT OF THE TIME

|     |     |     |     |
|-----|-----|-----|-----|
| 1.  | N   | 6.  | C   |
| 2.  | N   | 7.  | N   |
| 3.  | N   | 8.  | C   |
| 4.  | C   | 9.  | N   |
| 5.  | C   | 10. | C   |

C = 4 + 5 + 6 + 8 + 10 = 33

N = 1 + 2 + 3 + 7 + 9 = 22

# 2-90. SHOWING YOUR VERSATILITY

Answers will vary. These are suggestions.

1. (a) Ms. Sampson is a lawyer who questioned the frightened witness.

   (b) Questioning the witness, Ms. Sampson, a lawyer, frightened him or her.

2. (a) Justin went to the town meeting, became angry, and left after twenty minutes.

   (b) Justin, who went to the town meeting, became angry and left after twenty minutes.

   (c) When Justin went to the town meeting, he became angry and left after twenty minutes.

3. (a) Because Marie wanted to become an anthropologist, she studied hard.

   (b) Marie, who wanted to become an anthropologist, studied hard.

4. (a) When the box office opens at three o'clock, I will buy our concert tickets with my credit card.

   (b) Using my credit card, I will buy our concert tickets when the box office opens at three o'clock.

5. (a) I finished the easy puzzle in fifteen minutes.

   (b) The puzzle, which took me fifteen minutes to finish, was easy.